P9-DHS-277

# THE SERMON
# ON THE MOUNT

# THE SERMON
# ON THE MOUNT

BY

## W. D. DAVIES, M.A., D.D.

*George Washington Ivey Professor of Advanced Studies
and Research in Christian Origins,
The Divinity School, Duke University*

CAMBRIDGE
AT THE UNIVERSITY PRESS
1969

Published by the Syndics of the Cambridge University Press
Bentley House, 200 Euston Road, London N.W.1
American Branch: 32 East 57th Street, New York, N.Y.10022

© Cambridge University Press 1966

Library of Congress Catalogue Card Number: 66–17057

Standard Book Numbers:
521 04797 8 clothbound
521 09384 8 paperback

First published 1966
Reprinted 1969

Printed in Great Britain
at the University Printing House, Cambridge
(Brooke Crutchley, University Printer)

# PREFACE

An invitation to deliver the Reinicker Lectures at the Protestant Episcopal Theological Seminary, Alexandria, Virginia, has provided the occasion for setting forth in a more accessible and brief form the main lines of the argument of my work *The Setting of the Sermon on the Mount* (Cambridge, 1964). I recall with real pleasure and gratitude the warm reception given to the lectures and the courtesy extended to me by faculty and students alike during my visit. The present title is used merely for the sake of distinguishing this volume from the former, larger one.

Parts of the lectures were also delivered at the Theological School, Johnson C. Smith University, Charlotte, North Carolina, where I was again treated with every courtesy by faculty and students and accorded the most attentive and appreciative hearing.

I wish to thank my tutor assistant at Union Seminary, Mr E. Parish Sanders, now Assistant Professor of Religion at McMaster University, Hamilton, Ontario, for his ready help with the preparation of the manuscript for the press, for compiling the index, and for many other kindnesses.

There remains only to add that this volume was awarded a prize by The Christian Research Foundation for the year 1964–5, and I desire to express my gratitude to the Foundation for this honour.

W. D. D.

*3 February 1966*

# CONTENTS

# ABBREVIATIONS

CDC   *The Zadokite Documents*. Ed. Chaim Rabin (Oxford, 1954)

DSD   The Manual of Discipline

DSS   The Dead Sea Scrolls

*SM*   The Sermon on the Mount

Unless otherwise stated Biblical quotations are from *The Revised Standard Version of the Bible* (RSV).

# THE SETTING IN MATTHEW

The portion of the New Testament with which we shall be concerned in this book is Matt. v–vii, which is usually referred to as the Sermon on the Mount ( = *SM*). This has been variously assessed. Some have found in it a pernicious document which has wrought incalculable harm by presenting an utterly impossible ethic. Others have found in it the finest statement of the highest morality that mankind has known. Different as are these estimates, however, they share one common assumption, namely, that Matt. v–vii can be regarded as a single entity which has its own unified secret to reveal, and that this secret is the ethical teaching of Jesus of Nazareth. But it is this assumption that modern critical studies have made very difficult. The views propounded by scholars in our day about the contents and structure of Matt. v–vii seem to compel the conclusion that the whole section is merely a collection of unrelated sayings of diverse origins, a patchwork, which cannot possibly retain the pre-eminence once accorded to it as the authoritative source for the teaching of Jesus. Three disciplines are mainly responsible for this.

First, there is the influence of source criticism. Protestant scholars have generally held that behind the *SM*, as behind the rest of Matthew, there are three main sources upon which Matthew has drawn for his material; these are Mark, written probably in Rome after A.D. 65, another written or oral collection of the sayings of Jesus usually dated about A.D. 50, and referred to as Q, and, thirdly, a source named M, probably derived from the Church at Jerusalem. Material from all three, Mark,

Q, M, has been combined in the *SM* as elsewhere in Matthew. Moreover, the multiplicity of sources is not alone to be reckoned with. There are also different views as to the priority ascribed by Matthew to those which he employed. While most have held that he has fitted material from M into a framework provided by Q, others have argued that material from Q has been fitted by him into the framework supplied by M. In any case it is the patch-work-quilt character of the so-called 'sermon' that most forcibly emerges. And the question is inevitable, whether we can treat Matt. v–vii as a unity at all when it is so clearly an agglomeration of sources. At least, the section cannot be regarded as a 'sermon': at best it can only be a collection of sayings drawn from discourses uttered at divers times and circumstances. That these discourses necessarily go back to Jesus himself has been questioned in the light of the next discipline we have to notice.

Secondly, then, apart from the plague of source criticism, there is what has been called the 'nightmare of form criticism'. Before the tradition about what Jesus did and said came to be written in documents, it circulated for over two decades at least in an oral form. And, as its name suggests, form criticism has been concerned to examine the forms which the tradition about Jesus assumed in this period before it came to be recorded in writing. These forms have been variously classified, but a common conviction appears in most of the work of form critics, namely, that the tradition about Jesus was preserved, moulded, and, therefore, influenced by the Christian community. It was the needs of the Church in preaching, teaching, apologetic, propaganda, catechetical instruction at baptism and other occasions—it was all these that determined what was transmitted both in content and in form. Some form critics ascribe not only the preservation of the tradition but its very creation, in large measure, to the Church itself. In any case, it is only through the eyes of early Christians that we can see Jesus of Nazareth and through their ears only can we hear him. Thus form-criticism, just as it has invaded the quest of the historical Jesus to produce frequently a deep-seated scepticism as to the possibility of finding out what actually happened in the life of Jesus, has also influenced—not to say vitiated—efforts to establish the exact content of the teaching of Jesus. For example, Bultmann, one of the leading practitioners of form criticism, is compelled to reduce the *SM* to an arrangement of a multiplicity of pericopae or divisions of tradition which have assumed a certain form and whose contents are to be traced not to Jesus himself but to the early Church. Thus, like source criticism, form criticism has complicated attempts to understand Matt. v–vii as a totality by dividing it into small sections, the authenticity of which is very variously estimated.

And, thirdly, closely related to form criticism is the work of those scholars who have emphasized the liturgical factors in the formation of the Gospel tradition. According to these the tradition about Jesus took shape under the need to supply the Church with lectionary material, i.e., material that could be used in the services of the Church for reading in public. The work and words of Jesus were thus forced into a calendrical mould to fit the needs of each Sunday in the year; and the *SM* was probably formed as a lesson to be read at a particular time in the Church year. Quite clearly, it follows from this not only that it could be unwise to attach undue historicity to the sequence given to the life of Jesus in the Gospels, but, in particular for our purpose, that the material in the *SM* will have suffered considerable fashioning. It has been cut to size for use in public reading in the services of the Church.

We have above indicated the three main disciplines—source, form and liturgical criticism—which make the interpretation of Matt. v–vii as a unit very tortuous. Their impact is to cast doubt on the propriety of seeking to understand this section as an interrelated totality derived from the actual teaching of Jesus. Nor must this impact be ignored. Matt. v–vii *is* made up of material from diverse sources, which can fairly easily be isolated and can be seen tabulated in any handbook on the Gospels. The needs of the Church *have* dictated, if not created, much of the form and, probably, some of the contents of the material. Liturgical elements *have* undoubtedly crept into the section. By way of a single illustration let us compare the form of the Lord's Prayer as it occurs in Matthew and in Luke. They read as follows:

| Matt. vi. 9 ff.* | Luke xi. 1 ff |
|---|---|
| Our Father *which art in Heaven*, | And He was praying at a certain place and when he stopped, one of his disciples said to him, 'Lord teach us to pray, as John taught his disciples.' |
| Hallowed be Thy Name, | |
| Thy Kingdom come, | |
| *Thy Will be done*, | |
| *On earth as it is in Heaven*. | |
| Give us this day our daily bread | He said to them, When you pray say |
| And forgive us our trespasses | Father, hallowed be thy Name, |
| As we forgive those that trespass against us | Thy Kingdom come, |
| And lead us not into temptation | Give us this day our daily bread |
| *But deliver us from evil* | And forgive us our trespasses |
| *For thine is the Kingdom* | As we forgive those that trespass against us |
| *and the Power and the Glory* | And lead us not into temptation. |
| *for ever and ever. Amen.* | |

* The words italicized are best understood as liturgical formulations to make the prayer appropriate for public worship.

To impose a unity of a literary kind on Matt. v–vii is therefore erroneous. This is the weakness of two recent treatments of the sermon. Morton Smith of Columbia University has argued that the section is modelled on Rabbinic or Synagogal sermons, and Austin Farrer of Oxford University has found in it an intricate literary pattern. But from the purely literary point of view the *SM* is not impressive, and both these scholars have to force the evidence too much to be convincing.

Nevertheless—and this is to be emphasized—although it is possible with Morton Smith to carry the unity of the *SM* too far, and to demand of it a logical sermonic sequence which it is not its intention to provide, and, although Austin Farrer also goes too far in discovering a literary subtlety in the section, both Morton Smith and Farrer have helped us to recover an emphasis that recent criticism has tended to ignore. This emphasis is that we should think of Matthew, as of the other composers of the Gospels, not as mere editors, manipulating sources with scissors and paste, so to speak, to produce a mosaic of snippets, but as themselves in a real sense 'authors'. Dependent on a tradition they were, but they were not passive transmitters of it. By what they preserved, by the way they changed it and, above all, arranged it, they left their impress upon it. This is particularly true of Matthew. He (and by Matthew I refer to the 'school of Matthew' if such existed as well as to any single individual who may have been especially responsible for the Gospel), he himself was no unimaginative compiler or slavish editor: he himself was a formulator of the tradition, concerned to present it in a specific way to meet the needs of his Church, as he understood them. And in the light of this we must insist that Matthew, the final author of the Gospel (note we write '*author*' not '*editor*'), did himself regard v–vii as a unit. The concluding formula in vii. 28–9 makes this clear. The section finishes with the words: 'And it came to pass when Jesus had ended these sayings the people were astonished at his doctrine, for he taught them as one having authority and not as the scribes.' Matt. v–vii is not a sermon: Matthew has, however, used his sources for his own ends, so that v–vii do constitute for him an essential unity. Our first task, therefore, in our examination of the section is to ask what meaning it had for Matthew himself: how did he intend it to be understood?

How can we discover this? There are certain documents which are so loosely constructed that it is possible to treat their separate parts satisfactorily in isolation from the whole. Thus certain sections in Mark, perhaps, can be so treated. But there are other documents which are so closely knit that their parts are only adequately understood in the light of the whole. Such is the Fourth Gospel and such also is Matthew. It reveals a meticulous concern in the arrangement of its details and an architectonic grandeur in its totality: its different parts are inseparable, like those of a well-planned and well-built house. Any attempt, therefore, to understand the *SM* in stark isolation from the rest of the Gospel must be deemed inadequate: it must first be approached in its setting in the structure of Matthew as a whole.

## A. *The pentateuchal theory*

First, then, what is the structure of Matthew? A tradition going back to Papias (Bishop of Hierapolis in Asia Minor, who lived between *circa* 60 and 130 A.D.), in part at least, has been much revived in our time. The view has been urged that apart from the 'prologue' in i–ii, and the epilogue in xxvi–xxviii, the remainder of the material in the Gospel falls into five groups or books, as follows:

Preamble or prologue: i–ii: The birth narrative.

Book I: (a) iii. 1–iv. 25: Narrative material.
(b) v. 1–vii. 27: The Sermon on the Mount.
 Formula: vii. 28–9: '*And when Jesus finished these sayings*, the crowds were astonished at his teaching, for he taught them as one who had authority, and not as their scribes.'

Book II: (a) viii. 1–ix. 35: Narrative material.
(b) ix. 36–x. 42: Discourse on mission and martyrdom.
 Formula: xi. 1: '*And when Jesus had finished instructing his twelve disciples*...'

Book III: (a) xi. 2–xii. 50: Narrative and debate material.
(b) xiii. 1–52: Teaching on the Kingdom of Heaven.
 Formula: xiii. 53: '*And when Jesus had finished these parables*...'

Book IV: (a) xiii. 54–xvii. 21: Narrative and debate material.
(b) xvii. 22–xviii. 35: Discourse on church administration.
 Formula: xix. 1: '*Now when Jesus had finished these sayings*...'

Book V: (a) xix. 2–xxii. 46: Narrative and debate material.
(b) xxiii. 1–xxv. 46: Discourse on eschatology: farewell address.
 Formula: xxvi. 1: '*When Jesus finished all these sayings*, he said to his disciples...'

Epilogue: xxvi. 3–xxviii. 20: From the Last Supper to the Resurrection.

Each of the books, isolated in the above table, is closed by a formula which, as can be seen, occurs in almost identical forms at vii. 28, xi. 1, xiii. 53, xix. 1, xxvi. 1. And the five blocks of material naturally call to mind the five books of the Law at the beginning of the OT, namely, Genesis, Exodus, Leviticus, Numbers, Deuteronomy. The Law consists of these five books of the commandments of Moses: in each book each body of law is introduced by a narrative largely concerned with the signs and wonders which Jehovah had wrought in redeeming his people from Egypt. Roughly the same schematization appears in Matthew's Gospel. Each of his five books begins with an introductory narrative and closes with a stereotyped formula linking its discourse with the next narrative section. The suggestion is, therefore, natural that Matthew

was concerned to present his Gospel in the form of a new
Pentateuch, or a new book of the Law. And as a corollary
to this he thought of Jesus as a New Moses and of the
mount on which the Sermon was delivered as the counterpart of Mount Sinai from which the first Moses had given
both the written and the oral Law. Whether there was a
geographic mountain from which Jesus delivered one
massive discourse or from which He was accustomed
frequently to address his followers must remain an open
question. For Matthew himself, it is not the geographic
mountain that mattered but the mountain as a symbol of a
New Sinai from which the New Moses uttered his new law
or teaching.

There are difficulties in this theory which are too seldom
noticed. First, is it correct to assume that the words which
occur at the close of the five discourses constitute anything
more than a connecting formula, a merely literary link?
Perhaps the formula was insignificant in the mind of
Matthew and should not be given much weight in the
interpretation of his work. Secondly, it is possible that
Matthew derived this fivefold division from his sources.
Such a division is common in Jewish tradition. There are
five books of Psalms (i–xli; xlii–lxxii; lxxiii–lxxxix;
xc–cvi; cvii–cl); each of these five books ends with a formula of praise which, though not identical in each case,
is throughout comparable, for example, Ps. xli. 3 at the
end of Book I reads: 'Blessed be the Lord God of Israel
from everlasting and to everlasting. Amen, and Amen.'
Again lxxii. 18 at the end of Book III reads: 'Blessed be
the Lord God, the God of Israel, who only doeth won-
drous things.' Again, there are five divisions in Ecclesiasticus, five divisions in Proverbs, in I Enoch, and in the
original form of the Pirqe Aboth. It may therefore be that
the fivefold division was merely traditional and had no

profound significance for Matthew: it is a division of convenience, not of theological intention. And again, thirdly, any rigid parallelism between the arrangement of the material in Matthew and in the Pentateuch on examination breaks down. Had Matthew had a strictly detailed schematic parallelism with the Pentateuch in mind, it would have been far more obvious.

How shall we evaluate these difficulties in the pentateuchal theory of Matthew? The formula at the close of each discourse must, I think, be taken seriously: its regular introduction points to a peculiar import and its length gives it an unmistakable deliberateness; it does not seem to be a mere connecting link or a mere liturgical formula. As to the fivefold structure being a derivative merely borrowed by Matthew from his sources, it is difficult to find either in Q or M anything like a fivefold division. It is when we come to the third objection that we are on dangerous ground. The parallelism between Matthew and the five books of Moses can be overemphasized. On any theory of a detailed parallelism the first chapter of Matthew should correspond to Gen. i. 1. This is in fact the case, as we shall see below, on pages 12 ff.; but, on the theory of the five books with which we are dealing, Matt. i and ii are outside the parallelism. But this leads to the most serious difficulty for the theory. The birth narratives of Matt. i and ii, which constitute the prologue of the Gospel, and the story of the Passion and Resurrection, the epilogue of the Gospel, are placed outside its main structure. This would be grave enough did it only involve the prologue, the birth narratives, but it might be considered almost fatal when very probably, if not certainly, the most basic elements in the preaching of the early Church, the Death and Resurrection of Jesus, are treated as a kind of afterthought or addendum.

Thus, in view of the above difficulties, the five-book theory of Matthew—or the theory of its pentateuchal structure—taken alone, although highly attractive, remains questionable. We must therefore ask, before we accept or reject it, whether there are other elements in the Gospel which would suggest support for the theory. Are there sections pointing to the fact that for Matthew Jesus of Nazareth was the New Moses of a New Sinai?

## B.    *The New Moses*

Let us first look at the prologue of the Gospel, i.e., i and ii, what we call the Christmas story. These consist of the genealogy of Jesus, the account of the 'Virgin Birth', the visit of the wise men from the East, the flight to Egypt, because of the massacre of the innocents, and the return thence. As in the OT, so in the New the prologues to the various documents often illumine their contents. For example, in the book of Job the prologue telling about Satan's activity in going 'to and fro in the earth' is designed to make the reader aware of the real reason for Job's suffering, that is, the activity of Satan, even though this reason is hidden from the sufferer himself and from those around him. So, too, in the NT the prologues of Mark and the Fourth Gospel explain the theme of these two documents, while the prologue of Luke makes the author's aim quite explicit—it is to write in order and accurately the things concerning Jesus (Luke i. 1–4). We are, therefore, justified in suspecting that this might be the case in Matthew also. Indeed we might expect it to be pre-eminently true of this Gospel because of its so emphatic schematic character. We shall now inquire whether certain motifs which emerge in the Prologue might help us to understand the rest of the Gospel and especially the *SM*.

We shall here assume that the first two chapters of Matthew are not mere addenda to the Gospel and that the Gospel at no time circulated without them. The prologue constitutes a deliberate unit as an integral part of the Gospel. What are the motifs that govern the prologue? There are three ways in which we may approach this question. The prologue may be regarded as having a historical unity and may be deemed to be concerned with strictly biographical details. Again, its unity may be regarded as mythological or, again, its unity may be found in its interpretative or, to use a technical phrase, its *midrashic* character. That there is interpretation in the prologue few would deny. Can we disentangle this interpretation?

Some have held that an apologetic motif governs the chapters. Matthew's whole object was to show, in the face of current calumnies, that the Messiah's genealogy was divinely ordered and legally correct, while the story of the Virgin Birth is designed to meet Jewish calumny about the illegitimate birth of Jesus. But it is very doubtful whether the aim of combating Jewish calumnies on the birth of Jesus did play any significant part in the formation of the birth narratives. The calumnies belong to a later date. Nor must the possibility be ruled out that it was the birth narratives themselves that actually stimulated such calumnies. In any case, the motive of combating slanders against Mary's chastity is inadequate to explain the richness of the infancy narratives. When we pass to the story of the wise men and other events of ii, we find similar attempts made to explain them as aimed at enhancing the claims of Jesus in the Gentile world. This was the way in which many of the Fathers actually used the birth narratives. But here again it has to be recognized that these narratives could and did occasion difficulty. A

Church that had to combat astrological speculation would hardly present the story of the Star of Bethlehem as part of its apology: the birth narratives were a source of offence, because they placed Jesus, or so they could be interpreted, under the domination of the stars, a fact which Christians had to explain away.

In view of all this it is well not to overemphasize the strictly apologetic or polemic motifs in the birth narratives. They are probably directed, not to the world, but to the Church: they aim not at meeting calumnies and producing an impression upon the pagan world but at expounding the mystery of Christ, through his birth, to the Church itself. It is from this point of view that we shall now examine the Prologue. Three motifs seem to emerge in the infancy stories.

First, then, we note an interest in asserting that the coming of Jesus of Nazareth into history inaugurates a new era or a new creation. The very first verse of the Gospel begins: 'The book of the genealogy of Jesus Christ, the son of David, the son of Abraham.' The Greek of this verse, literally translated, means—'*the book of the genesis of Jesus Christ*'. This phrase has been variously translated and its significance is still disputed. Most recent scholars have regarded it as the title of the genealogical table or list that follows in i. 2–16: 'generation', '*genesis*', often means a genealogy. But there are two difficulties in this view. The phrase *the book of the generation* in the OT is usually followed by a list of descendants, not of progenitors or forefathers. Again, where it is used to introduce a genealogy, it occurs usually in the plural. I should like to suggest, therefore, that the term *genesis* is to be taken literally as 'generation' and is intended to refer us to the beginning of the OT, to the first book of Genesis, to the generation of the universe itself in Gen. i. 1–ii. 3 or to the creation or genesis of the first Adam in Gen. ii. 4 ff. (See Gen. ii. 4–v. 1 ff.). The evangelist has consciously begun his Gospel with a phrase intended to suggest a parallel between Jesus and the first Adam, and, even more, with the very creation of the universe. Matthew is concerned to assert in the prologue that the coming of Jesus was a new creation. The significance of the prologue is to suggest that the birth can be compared adequately only with the creation of the universe itself. The first phrase of Matthew is not a title for the genealogy only but for the whole Gospel of the new creation or the new Genesis.

This is reinforced by the story of the Virgin Birth, i. 18–25:

Now the birth of Jesus Christ took place in this way. When his mother Mary had been betrothed to Joseph, before they came together she was found to be with child of the Holy Spirit… '…that which is conceived in her is of the Holy Spirit;…'

The concept of the Holy Spirit is seldom mentioned in the Synoptic Gospels, but here it is prominent. The Holy Spirit is presented as the agent of Jesus' birth from Mary. Why? The association of the Holy Spirit with creation is made clear in Gen. i. 1 f.:

In the beginning God created the heavens and the earth. The earth was without form and void, and darkness was upon the face of the deep; and the Spirit of God was moving over the face of the waters.

Here the Spirit of God moves over material things, and it may be that we should not compare the activity of the Spirit in a living person, Mary, with the same activity on inanimate nature. But this is to be too precise. There can be little question that it is the thought of a new creation analogous with the first, in which the Spirit of God was active, which governs the role of the Spirit in Matt. i. 18–25. So, too, the use of the term Emmanuel in

i. 23, '"Behold, a virgin shall conceive and bear a son, and his name shall be called Emmanuel" (which means, God with us)'. This suggests the presence of the God who was active in creation and is now, through Jesus, with his people.

That the thought of Matthew turns to the creation of the world is again possibly implied by a certain parallelism between the opening of Matthew's Gospel and Gen. i and ii. Gen. i gives a catalogic account of the process which culminates in man's creation in the image of God. Gen. ii gives a more 'homely' description of the creation of man, providing a fairly detailed account of the actual creation. There is such a distinction in Matt. i and ii except that there the processes are reversed. First, in Matthew, we get a catalogue of ancestors culminating in the Jesus of history: the 'earthly' process of Christ's generation is, as it were, shown. Then in i. 18–25 we find a meticulous treatment of the way in which this man came into being: he proves to be the Son of God born of the Spirit from on high. Matthew, like Paul, deals first with the earthly Jesus in Matt. i. 1–17 and then in i. 18–25 points out his heavenly origin. Compare the words of Paul in 1 Cor. xv. 44*b*–47:

If there is a physical body, there is also a spiritual body. Thus it is written, 'The first man Adam became a living being'; the last Adam became a life-giving spirit. But it is not the spiritual which is first but the physical, and then the spiritual. The first man was from the earth, a man of dust; the second man is from heaven.

In the rest of the prologue we cannot trace the specific concept that Christ is the new creation, and so we pass on to the second motif, namely, that Jesus is the Son of David, the King Messiah. Here the possibilities are many. The genealogy in i is reckoned from Abraham to David, from David to the Exile, from the Exile to the New David, who is Jesus Christ. It is divided into three sections of fourteen generations each. The word David in Hebrew, if taken numerically, gives the figures $4+6+4 = 14$; and it is not impossible that the author of the Gospel intends us to see in the structure of the Genealogy an indication of Christ as the New David. More important, however, than this doubtful conjecture are the repeated references to David in the rest of the chapters. Thus in i. 20:

> ...an angel of the Lord appeared to him in a dream, saying, 'Joseph, son of David, do not fear to take Mary your wife...'

and in ii. 2, the wise men seek Jesus as the King of the Jews. Moreover, in the very first verse Jesus Christ is the Son of David. There can be little doubt, therefore, that the prologue sets forth Jesus both as the inaugurator of a new world or creation and as the Son of David, i.e., the Messianic King, the agent of the Messianic Age.

But there is another important motif to be discerned in the prologue. Jesus is still further the New Moses: a parallelism is drawn between his birth and that of Moses. And at this point it is impossible to exaggerate the significance that Moses had for Judaism. He was a veritable colossus, the mediator of the Law, which was regarded as the final revelation of God to man. To proclaim Jesus as a New Moses was to ascribe to him perhaps the highest honour that Judaism could offer. How does Matthew develop this theme? There is a possible parallel between Herod in the birth narratives and Pharaoh in the story of Moses: the massacres of the male children by the Pharaoh when the first Moses was born and by Herod when the New Moses was born are very similar. The flight into Egypt and the return thence, which ends with the words 'that it might be fulfilled which was spoken by the Lord, through the prophet saying, 'Out of Egypt did I call my son''' (Hos. xi. 1), at least imply a correspondence between the Exodus and the life of Jesus. That life recapitulates in itself the history of the people of Israel: he is Israel. Notice that here, therefore, the category of the New Moses must not be taken to exhaust the significance of the reference. The prologue does not elevate any one motif such as that of the New Moses into pre-eminence: it employs the various motifs in concert.

The same appears when we turn to the epilogue of Matthew, i.e. xxvi–xxviii. The story of the death of Jesus in Matthew does not add much to our purpose apart from the fact that, as in Mark and elsewhere in the NT, the narrative of the Last Supper recalls the Jewish Passover: xxvi. 26 ff.:

> Now as they were eating, Jesus took bread, and blessed, and broke it, and gave it to the disciples and said, 'Take, eat; this is my body.' And he took a cup, and when he had given thanks he gave it to them, saying,' Drink of it, all of you; for this is my blood of the covenant, which is poured out for many for the forgiveness of sins.'

The term 'covenant' in this context recalls the first covenant made at Sinai. For Matthew, as for the early Church generally, the Christian dispensation is a new Exodus wrought by Jesus as the New Moses. This apart, however, and it is of course a very important section, there is in the passion narrative of Matthew no emphasis on Christ as the New Moses. But there is perhaps a trace of his figure in Matt. xxviii. 16–20, the final resurrection scene. It reads:

> Now the eleven disciples went to Galilee, to the mountain to which Jesus had directed them. And when they saw him they worshiped him; but some doubted. And Jesus came and said to them, 'All authority in heaven and on earth has been given to me. Go therefore and make disciples of all nations, baptizing them in the name of the Father and of the Son and of the Holy Spirit, teaching them to observe all that I have commanded you; and lo, I am with you always, to the close of the age.'

The nature of this recital is important: it probably expresses the truth of the Resurrection and its meaning

for Matthew and is likely to reveal much about his understanding of the whole Gospel. He thinks of the Risen Lord
as the new lawgiver. First, there is the reference again to
the mountain. It raises the question as to the connotation
of the mountain here as in v. 1 and xvii. 1. Probably no
simple geographic mountain is intended. The mountain is
the mountain of the New Moses, the New Sinai. As in v. 1,
so here in xxviii. 16–20 the mountain seems to point us
back to the Old Sinai which is now superseded by a new.
Not all scholars accept this view, but it is not to be dismissed cavalierly. Secondly, the disciples are here sent
forth, among other things, to teach whatsoever Christ
has commanded. He is, in short, the source of the new
commandments under which the Church is to live. The
phrase 'whatsoever I have commanded you' points back
to Matt. v–vii where the words of Jesus are set alongside
those of Moses.

That the closing verses of Matthew's Gospel point us
back to the beginning of the Gospel also appears from the
third point to be noticed. The last words of xxviii. 20
read: '...and lo, I am with you always, to the close of the
age.' They recall the words in i. 23: 'And they shall call
his name Emmanuel, which being interpreted is, God
with us.' This reminiscence of the prologue in the epilogue
is not accidental, and we should be prepared to find traits
of the New Moses which we meet in the prologue paral-
leled in the epilogue.

But here again a caution is to be voiced. The 'New
Moses' motif is certainly not the sole and not the chief
element in the epilogue. The section points back even
more to the descriptions of the triumphant Son of Man in
Dan. vii; and pictures Jesus as the triumphant Son of Man
to whom all authority has already been given in heaven
and earth. Thus Jesus may be the New Moses in xxviii.

16–20 (the substance of such a figure is there, if not the name), but also someone else: the category of New Moses does not exhaust the significance of the Risen Lord.

## C. *New Exodus*

There would seem to be, then, some justification, to put it mildly, for finding in the Prologue and Epilogue support for the pentateuchal view of Matthew in so far as they represent Jesus as the New Moses. What of the rest of the Gospel? There are two other possibilities at least. First, in viii and ix of Matthew we find ten miracles performed by Jesus. They are:

> The cleansing of the leper;
> The healing of the centurion's servant ill with palsy;
> The healing of the mother-in-law of Peter;
> The stilling of the storm;
> The exorcising of devils into the Gadarene swine;
> The healing of the man sick of the palsy;
> The raising of the ruler's daughter from death;
> The healing of the woman with the issue of blood;
> The healing of two blind men;
> The casting out of a devil from a dumb man.

It has been claimed that the above ten miracles are meant to correspond antithetically to the ten plagues inflicted upon the Egyptians and the ten marvels wrought by Moses at the time of the first Exodus. This is in fulfilment of Mic. vii. 15: 'As in the days of thy coming forth out of the land of Egypt will I show unto him marvellous things.' But there are many difficulties in such a view. Not all have found ten miracles in viii–ix, but, even if it be admitted that there are, in fact, ten miracles in these chapters, do they suggest the Exodus? The figure of ten miracles—ten is a frequent enumeration in Jewish sources—may be purely accidental and may, therefore, have no theological or symbolic significance. Throughout the miracles it is not the activity of God in the Exodus that is recalled so much as the creative Word of Genesis i. 1 f. (see viii. 14, viii. 9, 13, viii. 28–34).

Throughout the section, in almost all its parts, we are recalled not so much to the Exodus as to Gen. i, and confronted with the succour of one who reminds us of the activity of God, by his word, in creation itself, and who is at the same time Son of Man (especially in viii. 18 ff.). Moreover, the whole series of miracles is brought to a close with words which are hardly appropriate if the intention were to draw a parallel between Jesus and Moses: they read, 'Never was anything like this seen in Israel' (ix. 33). And the very last words in ix. 34 may further indirectly confirm our refusal to see an Exodus motif in viii. 1–ix. 34. The sorcerers, etc., at the Exodus are led to recognize in the activity of Moses the finger of God (Exod. viii. 19), but the Pharisees only see in that of Jesus a sign that he is the Prince of demons. Matthew does not here rebut the charge, but he does so elsewhere in terms which are, for our purpose, highly significant. Compare the following verses from Luke xi. 19 ff. and Matt. xii. 27 ff. where the rebuttal occurs:

| Luke | Matthew |
|---|---|
| And if I cast out demons by Beelzebul, by whom do your sons cast them out? Therefore they shall be your judges. But if it is by *the finger of God* that I cast out demons, then the kingdom of God has come upon you. | And if I cast out demons by Beelzebul, by whom do your sons cast them out? Therefore they shall be your judges. But if it is by *the Spirit of God* that I cast out demons, then the kingdom of God has come upon you. |

Luke's version is probably the more original. In any case, whereas Luke understands the exorcistic work of Jesus in the light of the Exodus, Matthew, who may have deliberately altered Q, connects it with the Spirit active in the creation as described in Gen. i. 1. This difference between Luke and Matthew indicates that creation motifs were as strong as those of the Exodus in Matthew. Luke elsewhere has an interest in the Spirit.

In one section in Matthew, however, we may be fairly certain that the motif of the New Exodus is present and, probably, emphasized. This section is that dealing with the Transfiguration of Jesus (see Mark ix. 2–8; Matt. xvii. 1–8; Luke ix. 28–36). Here we find a more tangible indication of Matthew's interest in the Exodus motif. All three of the Synoptic accounts have been claimed to present Jesus in the light of the Exodus and of the first Moses at this point. In the Marcan account, which lies behind Matthew, the following have been alleged as indications of this:

(a) In ix. 2 the phrase 'after six days' is symbolic. As in Exod. xxiv. 16 Moses was commanded by the Lord to build the Tabernacle, so the three who accompany Jesus on the Mount of Transfiguration are led after six days to build tents (ix. 5).

(b) The voice of God is uttered from the midst of the cloud (Exod. xxiv. 15 ff. and Mark ix. 7), just as the command came to Moses on a mountain covered by 'the cloud'.

(c) Just as in Exod. xxiv. 1 f. Moses is accompanied by a small group, Aaron, Nadab, Abihu, and the seventy elders, while the people as a whole are kept at the foot of the mountain, so Jesus is accompanied by Peter, James and John, while the rest of the disciples and the crowds remain below. On Sinai, Moses alone, and on the Mount of Transfiguration, Jesus alone, holds converse with the Lord, or is in intimacy of fellowship with the Unseen.

(d) Noteworthy is it that the two figures who appear

along with Jesus on the Mount are those of two men who held discourse with God on Mount Sinai: Moses in Exod. xxxiii. 17 ff., and Elijah in 1 Kings xix. 9–13. They now appear, so we are perhaps meant to think, on a New Sinai.

(e) The radiance of Moses on his descent from Mount Sinai (Exod. xxxiv. 29 ff.) may be recalled in Mark ix. 2, 'and he was transfigured before them and his garments became glistening, intensely white, as no fuller on earth could bleach them'.

(f) In Mark ix. 7 the command is issued to obey Jesus, even as Moses was obeyed. The verse may recall Deut. xviii. 15, Jesus being the prophet like unto Moses.

The emphasis in Mark does not lie there. The mere fact that Mark alone places Elijah before Moses indicates this. Briefly, the Transfiguration scene in Mark is probably best understood in relation to Mark's emphasis on the Passion, which has preceded it. Jesus, destined to suffer, nevertheless, at the Transfiguration, is proclaimed as Messiah, Servant, Son of Man: the proclamation at the Baptism is now enhanced—Jesus is Son of Man after the manner of the Book of Daniel. Thus the Transfiguration looks forward in Mark both to the Passion and to the Resurrection. This appears from the insistence on the Cross of the Son of Man (ix. 12); the priority given to Elijah, who is identified with the Baptist, whose death was a premonition of that of Jesus himself (ix. 12); the similarity between the Transfiguration and the Agony in Gethsemane, in that the witnesses of both are identical (ix. 12; xiv. 33); and the metamorphosis of Jesus in ix. 2 which looks forward to the glory of the Resurrection (xvi. 12) (cf. 1 Pet. i. 16–18). All this does not mean that the figure of Moses has not influenced Mark's account of the Transfiguration. Clearly Jesus is both distinguished

from Moses, who along with Elijah testifies by his presence
to him, and also set in parallelism to him, as the prophet
like unto him. Nevertheless, even in this parallelism there
may be a distinction: the content of the teaching of Jesus
in Mark ix. 30–2 is the suffering of the Son of Man, not
ethical commandments. (But these, though not expressly
mentioned, should not perhaps be excluded from the
provenance of 'Hear ye Him', so that this last point cannot
be pressed.) In any case, not as 'Mosaic' teacher but as
suffering and triumphant Lord does Mark present Jesus
in the Transfiguration.

We may now ask how Matthew has dealt with Mark's
account. We have to notice significant changes in details
and in order.

(a) He alters Mark's order by referring to Moses before
referring to Elijah (xvii. 3). This is not a triviality. It at
least means that no priority of significance is given to
Elijah, as in Mark, and, probably, that the reference to
Moses is to be taken as emphatic.

(b) While Mark only refers to 'the garments of Jesus',
which became glistening, intensely white 'as no fuller on
earth could bleach them' (Mark ix. 3), Matthew adds:
'*and his face shone like the sun*' (xvii. 2). This recalls Exod.
xxxiv. 29–35, where the Hebrew reads: 'the skin of
[Moses'] face shone' because he had been talking to God
—there is no midrashic or haggadic ornamentation of
the phenomenon in Matthew, as in the rabbis. One fact
only concerns him, that on the face of Jesus is seen the
glory of the mediator of the Law, Moses (and this in later
rabbinic tradition is none other than the glory of the
Law itself).

(c) In describing 'the cloud' that appears, Matthew
uses the same verb as Mark and Luke, *overshadow*. But he
adds a significant adjective. The cloud is a 'bright' cloud:

thus he expresses a paradox, a bright light *overshadows*. Can we detect why he adds this adjective? Is it not to make it beyond doubt that he has the Shekinah in mind, that presence of the Lord which used to fill the tabernacle in the wilderness, and which was often connected with depths of light 'more intense than the midsummer sun'?

(*d*) The climax of the story is particularly instructive in Matthew. First, the declaration 'This is my beloved son, with whom I am well pleased' in Matt. xvii. 5 is significantly different from Mark ix. 35: 'This is my beloved Son', and from Luke: 'This is my Son, my Chosen.' Mark and Luke look back mainly to Ps. ii. 7, whereas Matthew here, as in the account of Jesus' baptism, refers to both Ps. ii. 7 and Isa. xlii. 1. 'Behold, my servant, whom I uphold, my chosen, in whom my soul delights...' Matthew seems to have added the phrase 'with whom I am well pleased' to signify Jesus as the one who was destined to bring his law to the nations (Isa. xlii. 4). Taken in isolation this suggestion cannot be pressed because the phrase 'with whom I am well pleased' is not a direct quotation of Isa. xlii. 1; but, on the other hand, other elements in the climax might support it. Thus, secondly, the final utterance of the Voice from heaven is a command to obey Jesus as God's Son. In Matthew there can be little doubt on *a priori* grounds that this points to Jesus as an ethical teacher, like Moses. Thus while the content of Jesus' teaching in Mark ix. 30–2 is explicitly stated as the suffering of the Son of Man, and this receives adequate recognition in Luke ix. 43*b*–45, Matthew, although he knows of the significance of the Passion, has so softened and shortened his reference to it in xvii. 22–3 that he has robbed it of its total pre-eminence. A comparison of the passages puts this beyond doubt:

Matt. xvii. 22–3:

As they were gathering in Galilee, Jesus said to them, 'The Son of man is to be delivered into the hands of men, and they will kill him, and he will be raised on the third day.' And they were greatly distressed.

Mark ix. 30–2:

They went on from there and passed through Galilee. And he would not have any one know it; for he was teaching his disciples, saying to them, 'The Son of man will be delivered into the hands of men, and they will kill him; and when he is killed, after three days he will rise.' But they did not understand the saying, and they were afraid to ask him.

Luke ix. 43 b–45:

But while they were all marvelling at everything he did, he said to his disciples, 'Let these words sink into your ears; for the Son of man is to be delivered into the hands of men.' But they did not understand this saying, and it was concealed from them, that they should not perceive it; and they were afraid to ask him about this saying.

In a similar spirit, it would seem that Matthew, after relating the Transfiguration, cannot quickly enough get to the discourse section, giving the teaching of Jesus, in xvii. 24–xviii. 35: he is concerned not primarily with the Passion motif after the Transfiguration but with the 'teaching' of Jesus (although he follows Mark too faithfully to omit that motif altogether, because it was too well fixed in the tradition here to be ignored). The 'Hear ye him' of xvii. 5 both looks backward to v–vii and forward to xvii. 5–xviii. 35. And it is possible, and even probable, that we should understand the phrase in the light of Deut. xviii. 15: 'The Lord shall raise up for you a prophet like me from among you, from your brethren—him shall ye heed' (compare xviii. 15); the future tense has become a present tense. But, thirdly, while Moses' figure informs so much in the Transfiguration scene, it is also no less surely being superseded. At the last, Moses and Elijah disappear and Jesus remains alone. This fact, common to all the Synoptics, is specifically emphasized by Matthew. Jesus, for Matthew, has become the teacher unique, the 'New Moses'. And, finally, it is important to note a change that Matthew has introduced in the order of the material at this point, in a section far too summarily dismissed by most commentators. Mark places the 'awe' felt by the disciples early in the narrative, immediately after the transfiguration of Jesus and the vision vouchsafed to them of Elijah and Moses—in that order—with him. Not the fact that he was to command, but that he was 'transfigured', is emphasized. Luke makes the descent of 'the cloud' the cause for fear (ix. 34 *b*). With Matthew it is otherwise. He reserves the expression of 'awe' in Peter and James and John till immediately after the words 'Hear ye him'. And it is such 'awe' as fells them to the ground: in token of their veneration they fall on their faces to the earth, as was customary in epiphanies (see Gen. xvii. 3, Abraham before God; 1 Sam. xxiv. 9, David before Saul; 2 Sam. ix. 6, Mephibosheth, son of Jonathan, before David; Dan. x. 9, Daniel before 'one in the likeness of the sons of men'). And the final item in the complex is that Jesus touches the disciples and says, 'Rise and have no fear.'

Our examination of the Transfiguration is over. Here more convincingly than in any other of the materials that we have so far examined Matthew seems to have altered and rearranged the material in Mark, not merely from motives of simple reverence (as in the use of 'Lord' in xvii. 4 rather than the *Rabbi* of Mark ix. 5 and the *Master* of Luke ix. 33, and the addition of 'if you wish' in xvii. 4 instead of the less polite 'let us make' of Mark ix. 5), but with the deliberate purpose of presenting Jesus after the manner of Moses, albeit a Moses whom he supersedes as 'the unique and definitive teacher of mankind'. (It is this Mosaic, and yet more than Mosaic, character of Matthew's Jesus that lies behind the substitution of 'Lord' for 'rabbi' at xvii. 4.)

Our examination thus indicates that Matthew was well aware of that interpretation of Christ which found his prototype in Moses, and that, at certain points, he may have allowed this to colour his Gospel. But the restraint with which the New Exodus and New Moses motifs are used is noticeable. Evidences for these two motifs are not sufficiently dominant to add any significant support to Bacon's pentateuchal hypothesis, which must, there-fore, still remain questionable, though possible. While these motifs have influenced Matthew's Gospel, it is not clear that they have entirely fashioned or moulded it. This also appears when we consider Matt. v–vii. Those elements to which we referred above, especially in the prologue and the Transfiguration, do add force to the view that in the *SM* we are to detect a New Sinai. But the tentativeness and reserve of Matthew's use of the Exodus motif is striking. There is no explicit reference to Mount Sinai; no features from the account of the giving of the Law in Exod. xix, as they are developed, for example, in Heb. xii. 18 ff., appear in v. 1 f.; and at no point, apart from the express quotations from the Law in the anti-theses in v. 21 ff., are we directly referred to the events at Sinai. Any pointers to the latter are extremely hesitant, if they exist at all. Even though the writing of a Gospel did not allow the same freedom of elaboration as did that of an epistle, like Hebrews, we cannot but ask whether Matthew could not have been somewhat bolder in his 'Mosaism' had the idea of a New Moses played a great part in his purpose in writing the Gospel. The case would seem to be that, while the category of a New Moses and a New Sinai is present in v–vii, as elsewhere in Matthew, the strictly Mosaic traits in the figure of the Matthaean Christ, both there and in other parts of the Gospel, have been taken up into a deeper and higher context. He is not Moses come as Messiah, if we may so put it, so much as Messiah, Son of Man, Emmanuel, who has absorbed the Mosaic function. The Sermon on the Mount is therefore ambiguous: suggestive of the Law of a New Moses, it is also the authoritative word of the Lord, the Messiah: it is the Messianic Torah.

## D. *Mosaic Categories Transcended*

But an adequate appreciation of the *SM* as Mosaic and yet more than Mosaic, that is, as Messianic Torah, can only be achieved when we ask two further questions. First, what is its relation to the moral demand as Matthew presents it elsewhere in the Gospel and, secondly, what precisely do the literary 'formulae' within the *SM* itself suggest as to its character'?

In answer to the first question it is clear that the Christian life for Matthew is a life of discipleship or learning under the yoke of Christ (xi. 29). The Church is a company of disciples (xiii. 52, xxiii. 8, xxviii. 20) who recognize prophets, wise men, scribes (xxiii. 34): it is a school of Christ's culture exercising the right of binding and loosing (xviii. 18), that is, of legislating conduct. Christians stand under the 'New Sinai' of a New Moses. But their relationship to this New Moses must be carefully noted. The Law which they obey is personalized in Jesus in a way in which the Law of Judaism was never personalized in Moses (vii. 24). And all Christian living is so personalized: it is above all a life of 'faith' in Jesus (xxiii. 23), a life of following him (xix. 16–20). And this implies the imitation of Christ, not in a wooden, literalistic sense, but in that the marks of the life of Jesus are to be traceable in that of his followers. Thus, in his counsels to the Twelve in Matt. x, Jesus seems to predicate of the life of his apostles what became true of himself in the Passion. And other similar marks of his life, apart from the Passion, strictly so called, are to characterize Christians—readiness to suffer (x. 17 ff.; xvi. 24 ff.), to be poor (xix. 23 ff.; vi. 19 ff.), to be humble (xviii. 1 ff.), to love (xxiii. 31 ff.), to reject worldly honour (xxiii. 7 ff.), to serve (xx. 20 ff.). Thus the ethical norm for Christians is not only the words but the life also of him who uttered them. The shadow of Jesus' own life is over all the Sermon. And, finally, we must go further. Jesus is never merely teacher for Matthew: the regular title he uses for Jesus is 'Lord'. In fact, Jesus is called rabbi or teacher only by Judas Iscariot. The purely Mosaic or didactic function of Jesus is transcended. True, Christians are disciples of Christ but they are such within the larger context of incorporation in Jesus and worship of him as their Lord. There is a kind of identity between the Matthaean Christian and his Lord which is not unlike the understanding of Christians as being 'in Christ' which we find in Paul (x. 40, xviii. 5, xv. 31 ff., xxv. 30–46). It is clear that the context of the *SM* in the totality of the Gospel's thought on the nature of the Christian life forbids any exclusive or even predominant 'Mosaic' approach to it: the Matthaean Jesus is never merely a teacher.

Turning to the nature of the terminology employed by Matthew to set forth the *SM*, one thing is highly significant. Mark (i. 21–8) had referred to the teaching of Jesus as New Teaching. But Matthew in reproducing Mark avoided this phrase. This means that for him the

teaching of Jesus was no revolutionary phenomenon: it
was not radically 'new'. This fact is confirmed by the
well-known verses in v. 17–20:

'Think not that I have come to abolish the law and the prophets; I
have come not to abolish them but to fulfil them. For truly, I say
to you, till heaven and earth pass away, not an iota, not a dot, will
pass from the law until all is accomplished. Whoever then relaxes one
of the least of these commandments and teaches men so, shall be
called least in the kingdom of heaven; but he who does them and
teaches them shall be called great in the kingdom of heaven. For I tell
you, unless your righteousness exceeds that of the scribes and Pharisees, you will never enter the kingdom of heaven.'

The Law remains in force. It is true that the so-called
Antitheses in v. 21–48 seem to annul parts of the Law, but
the meaning of these Antitheses has to be carefully
observed. The fact is that in none of the Antitheses is there
an intention to annul the provisions of the Law but only
to carry them out to their ultimate meaning. Daube has
expressed the matter as follows:

'...the Matthaean form is far milder, less revolutionary, than one
might incline to believe...these declarations, "Ye have heard—But
I say unto you", are intended to prove Jesus the Law's upholder, not
destroyer. The relationship between the two members of the form
is not one of pure contrast; the demand that you must not be angry
with your brother is not thought of as utterly irreconcilable with the
prohibition of killing. On the contrary, wider and deeper though it
may be, it is thought of as, in a sense, resulting from and certainly
including the old rule; it is the revelation of a fuller meaning for a new
age. The second member unfolds rather than sweeps away the first.'

To interpret on the side of stringency is not to annul the
Law, but to change it in accordance with its own intention.
From this point of view, as Daube shows, we cannot speak of
the Law being anulled in the antitheses, but only of its being
intensified in its demand, or reinterpreted in a higher key.

   This approach to Matthew's understanding of the Law
is confirmed when we examine the three passages where
the question of Jesus' attitude to the Law arises with

special force, that is, in Matt. xii. 1–14 where the observance of the Sabbath is discussed; in xv. 1–20 dealing
with the laws of purity and in xix. 1–19 dealing with
divorce. In all these three passages Matthew makes it
clear that the teaching of Jesus is not in antithesis to the
written Law of Moses, though it is critical of the oral
tradition: it is the full interpretation of the former, rather
than its annulment. It agrees with all this that throughout
Matthew the commandment of Moses remains the commandment of God. (Compare Mark vii. 10 and Matt.
xv. 4; Mark xii. 26 and Matt. xxii. 31. Jesus is not set in
opposition to Moses, whose words remain those of God.)
Similarly those in Israel who were especially regarded as
the interpreters of Moses are not dismissed outright by
Matthew: their practice he condemns but not their
teaching. This emerges in the well-known passages
xxiii. 1–7, and in xv. 1 ff., again, the adherence of the
Pharisees to the Law of Moses as such is not condemned,
but only their misinterpretation of it. The understanding
of the Law of Moses both within and without the *SM* in
Matthew forbids any emphasis on an antithesis to the
Law of Moses and must be allowed, along with the other
factors mentioned above, to temper an eagerness to see in
the Matthaean Jesus a New Moses opposed to the first.

The threads of our treatment must now be drawn together. That we might the better understand it, we have
sought, as pertinently as possible, to place the *SM* in its
setting within the Gospel as a whole. Matthew has been
shown to reveal the influence of the New Exodus and New
Moses motif, but this has not been allowed to dictate his
presentation of the Gospel to any serious degree. Thus
its fivefold structure cannot certainly be held to have any
theological significance, that is, it does not necessarily

point to a deliberate interpretation of the Gospel in terms of a new Pentateuch as, in its totality, a counterpart to the five books of Moses. At this point, though certainly not at others, it might prove profitable to exorcize the awe-inspiring ghost of Bacon from Matthaean studies. Similarly the *SM* itself is not set forth as a 'new', revolutionary Law, in sharp antithesis to that given on Sinai. Matthew, indeed, seems pointedly to have avoided the use of the phrase 'new teaching' to describe the words of Jesus and presents them as the true interpretation of the Law of Judaism. Not antithesis but completion expresses the relationship between the Law of Moses and the teaching of Jesus.

But the mere recognition of this is not enough: its full force for the understanding of Matthew must be apprehended. One of completion (reformation is too weak a word) and not revolution, the above relationship may be for him; but, quite clearly, he has, with unmistakable deliberateness and with massive and majestic impressiveness, placed the teaching of Jesus in the forefront of his Gospel. His Christ is inevitably thought of as on the Mount, a teacher of righteousness. At the same time the demand that Matthew's Christ laid upon his disciples, elsewhere in the Gospel, had a personal reference to himself, which could not be exhausted in terms of the commandments of the Sermon, but which, combined with the latter, make of it an expression of the Lord's very being. Despite its didactic isolation, its setting in Matthew's interpretation of the Gospel as a whole gives to the Sermon a quality of 'personalism' 'in Christ'. We cannot doubt that Matthew intended it to represent the Messianic Torah. By this he meant not a new, that is, a different, Law, but a new interpretation of the Old Law. This new interpretation of Jesus we can justifiably designate as

'Torah', just as the interpretations of Hillel and Shammai
are so designated (Tos. So. xiv. 9). But though strictly
interpretation, the words of Jesus are authoritative in a
new way (vii. 28). Daube, who more than any other has
taught us caution in applying the term 'antitheses' to the
demands of the *SM*, has also recognized the element of
newness in the words of Jesus.

The point is that, in Matthew, we have before us, not a scholarly
working out by some rabbis of a progressive interpretation as against
a conceivable narrow one, but a laying down by Jesus, supreme
authority, of the proper demand as against a view, be it held by
friends or enemies, which would still take the exact words of the
scriptural precept as a standard of conduct. Jesus, supreme authority,
lays down the proper demand: this accounts for 'But I say unto you,
That whosoever is angry, etc....'. The demand is opposed to a view
held among those addressed which would still take the exact words
of a precept as a basis: this accounts for, 'Ye have understood literally
what was said', etc. The setting in life of the rabbinic form is dialectic
exposition of the Law; that of the Matthaean is proclamation of the
true Law...

We cannot then doubt that the *SM* is the 'law' of Jesus
the Messiah and Lord. Our treatment thus ends in an
ambiguity. Matthew presents Jesus as giving a Messianic
Law on a Mount, but he avoids the express concept of a
New Torah and a New Sinai: he has cast around his Lord
the mantle of a teacher of righteousness, but he avoids the
express ascription to him of the honorific 'a New Moses'.
Can we understand this ambiguity? Why, in a Gospel
where there is much to evoke the use of these terms, where
the *substance* of the New Law, the New Sinai, the New
Moses, is present, is there an obvious hesitancy in giving
explicit expression to them? Perhaps the eschatological
expectations of and conditions within first-century Judaism can clarify this ambiguity and explain Matthew's
caution: we shall explore them in this hope in the next
two chapters.

# 2

# THE SETTING IN JEWISH
## MESSIANIC EXPECTATION

In the previous chapter we asserted that the view that
Matthew has divided his gospel into five books to correspond to the five books of the Law, so that for him Jesus
as presented in the *SM* is a New Moses giving his New
Law from the New Sinai by itself, taken in isolation, must
be questioned. There are, however, in the birth stories and
the epilogue of the Gospel, and possibly in the ten miracles
in viii and ix and in the story of the Transfiguration,
elements that tend to suggest that view even when they
make no explicit claim for it. Nevertheless, we may well
ask: is not all this very fanciful? The evidence may be
interpreted differently. The parallelism between Christ
and Moses is never explicitly drawn. Not even in the
prologue in ii. 15 can we, without any doubt, pin down
this correspondence. And even if it be claimed that we
could do so there, nevertheless the New Moses motif is not
found neat nor even predominant even there. As we saw,
it falls within a context which, like the other material
examined, emphasizes the advent of Christ as the in-
auguration of a new creation, the arrival of the Messianic
King, and, finally, the triumphant Son of Man. Moreover, can we really compare the role of Jesus on the mount
with that of Moses on Sinai? Moses was there a mediator
of the Law which he had received from God. Jesus, on the
other hand, in the *SM* either gives a new law or a new
interpretation of the Law and that on his own authority.
Similarly, if there be a parallel between Jesus and Moses
in xxviii. 16–20, there is also a contrast. Moses did not

enter into the land of promise; but Jesus, the Risen Lord of Matthew, already possesses the land: 'All power' has already been given to him. Furthermore, even if we admit the presence of the New Moses motif in Matthew, we saw that, so far from exhausting the Matthaean Christ, it is almost secondary. This comes out most clearly in xviii. 20 which reads, 'For where two or three are gathered together in my name there am I in the midst of them.' Here Christ himself fulfils the function of the Divine Presence. He is more than the new Moses: he symbolizes the Shekinah, the very presence of God itself. For Matthew, however much Jesus was the New Moses, he was also incomparable: of his word and deed he says, 'Any thing like this has not happened hitherto in Israel.'

What, then, justifies us, in view of these difficulties, in still maintaining that for Matthew the *SM* is the Law of the New and greater Moses, who is the Messiah, that is, the Messianic Law? To answer this question requires an act of imagination, the attempt to think in the terms in which those who lived in Palestine in the first century thought. To put the matter briefly, Judaism was governed by a memory and an anticipation: for Jewry the future was dictated by the past. First-century Judaism looked back and looked forward: what it saw in the past coloured its vision of the future: the future, indeed, was to be the past on a grander and more glorious scale. Memory and anticipation were the two poles of Jewish religious thought. And this was particularly true in the Messianic thinking of the time of Jesus. The Jews looked forward to a future when God would assert his sovereignty and, instead of the woes of the present, there would come the blessings of the ideal future. This was variously conceived. It would either be an earthly paradise introduced by an earthly human figure of the stock of David, the Messiah,

or, again, it might be a supernatural state of affairs introduced by a superhuman figure, the Son of Man. There
was no single Jewish expectation. A multiplicity of concepts jostled each other in the popular and learned mind.
But one thing did mark the expectations: the end would
be as the beginning. And so the Messiah, when he came,
would be like the great figures of the past. And who were
the great figures of Jewish history? Two, at least, David,
the king who had most extended Israel's frontiers, and
Moses, who had given to Israel its Law. The prophet who
was to arise at the end of the days was to be like unto
Moses. The ideal figure of the future would correspond
to the ideal figure of the past.

It is in the light of this Jewish expectation that we are
to understand Matthew's understanding of Jesus; and
especially, for our purpose, his understanding of Jesus as
the new and greater Moses. *This was the natural way for a
religious Jew in the first century to express his conviction and that
of his Church that Jesus of Nazareth was the ultimate figure, the
agent of the ideal future.* To regard Jesus as the New Moses
was to declare him the eschatological person, the person   *NB*
of the End.

But our concern with the *SM* prompts a further question. As we have seen, although he thinks of Jesus as the
Messiah and suggests that he is the New Moses, Matthew
expressly avoids describing the moral demands of Jesus
as a New Law or Teaching. Why? It is our suggestion that
one reason for this is that he was sensitive to Judaism and
to the Messianic expectations of his own people, the Jews.
The ambiguity of Jewish expectations has invaded
Matthew's text. To make clear what this means, let us
examine the way in which Judaism thought of the role
of the Law in the Messianic Age.

## A.  *The Old Testament*

The Old Testament knows of the expectation of a Messianic Age when things would be radically changed and become new. Did it expect the Law to become new in that age? The following passages are pertinent.

(1)  *Jer.* xxxi. 31–4:

Behold, the days are coming, says the Lord, when I will make a new covenant with the house of Israel and the house of Judah, not like the covenant which I made with their fathers when I took them by the hand to bring them out of the land of Egypt, my covenant which they broke, though I was their husband, says the Lord. But this is the covenant which I will make with the house of Israel after those days, says the Lord: I will put my law within them, and I will write it upon their hearts; and I will be their God, and they shall be my people. And no longer shall each man teach his neighbor and each his brother, saying, 'Know the Lord,' for they shall all know me, from the least of them to the greatest, says the Lord; for I will forgive their iniquity, and I will remember their sin no more.

The significant factors are the following. For Jeremiah the relation between Yahweh and his people in 'the days to come' will be covenantal: the covenant which will then come into being will be a new one: one element in it, as in all covenants, will be Torah. But, whereas in previous covenants the Torah involved was written on some outward material, and, in the particular covenant which Jeremiah had in mind, written on tablets of stone, in the new covenant the Torah will be written 'in the heart', or 'in the inward parts'; and whereas the writing of the previous Torah was accomplished by human means, the Torah in the new covenant will not need to be taught by human teachers, because all who participate in the new covenant will 'know' the Lord; and they will share in this knowledge because the barrier to it, sin, has been forgiven by God. As a result of all this, Israel will become the people of Yahweh and he their God.

Our main concern is with the Torah which Yahweh will write in the 'inward parts', or 'in the hearts' of his people.

It is possible to argue that the covenant envisaged by Jeremiah in the future would be a new covenant demanding a new kind of Torah, apparently of a kind which may best perhaps be called 'pneumatic' in the sense that it involved the activity of an inner, spontaneous principle. At the same time, however, there is reason to question that sharp antithesis to the old written Torah which this has been claimed to imply. We have to recognize a certain tension in his thought between the written Torah and the Torah to be dispensed in the 'New Covenant', and we cannot resolve this tension into a complete difference. What we are concerned to emphasize is that Torah, new in some sense and yet not divorced utterly from the Old Torah, that is, an external Torah, is part of Jeremiah's hope for 'the latter days'. For Jeremiah the New Covenant would probably demand both the letter and the Spirit.

## (2) *The Servant of the Lord and his Law*

There emerges in Deutero-Isaiah (at xlii. 1–4, xlix. 1–6, l. 4–11, lii. 13–liii. 12) a figure named the Servant of the Lord. The figure has been variously interpreted as referring to Israel as a whole, an ideal Israel within the people as a whole, and an individual. Some have seen in the Servant both a corporate and an individual figure. What is significant, for our purposes, is that the early Church ascribed this title to Jesus (Acts viii. 3–52; 1 Pet. ii. 21–3), that is, they identified the Messiah with the Servant. It is possible that this identification had already been made in the Old Testament.

It is striking that the Servant of the Lord in the Old Testament is a teacher of law. This can be stated particularly in view of the first of the Servant poems found in

xlii. 1–4. C. R. North renders it as follows in his work
*The Suffering Servant in Deutero-Isaiah* (London, 1948):

> Behold! My Servant whom I uphold,
> My chosen in whom I delight!
> I have endowed him with my spirit,
>
> He shall announce judgement to the nations,
> He shall not cry nor make any clamour,
> Nor let his voice be heard in the street;
>
> A reed that is bruised he shall not break,
> And the wick that burns dimly he shall not quench,
> Faithfully shall he announce judgement,
>
> Not burning dimly nor himself being bruised,
> Until he have established judgement in the earth.
> And for his instruction the far coasts wait eagerly.

The Hebrew term translated 'instruction' by North in
xlii. 4 is *torah*, usually rendered by 'law'. There is a clear
reference to the Law of the Servant. Perhaps the possessive
pronoun 'his law' emphasizes that the isles are waiting
for a Special Law which the Servant is to bring. The
imparting of Torah (Law) is a central function of the
Servant of the Lord: this Torah will be directed to the
world. It agrees with this that the traits of a 'teacher'
emerge clearly in the Servant. The following are the main
indications of this: like the prophets, the Servant is endowed with the Spirit (xlii. 1); he delivers Torah (xlii. 4);
he is a disciple either of another prophet or of one endowed
with the Spirit of God (i. 4); he has been called from his
mother's womb to his task, as were other prophets
(Jer. i. 5); he opens his ears daily for revelations (i. 4) and
it is by his message, as well as by his suffering, that he
works salvation (Isa. xlii. 4).

If the Servant had been identified with the Messiah
in the Old Testament, then the Messianic Age was conceived as one marked by his Torah or Law.

(3) *Isa. ii. 1–5* (with parallel, offering from our point of view only unimportant variation, in Mic. iv. 1–5):

> It shall come to pass in the latter days
>> that the mountain of the house of the LORD
> shall be established as the highest of the mountains,
>> and shall be raised above the hills;
> and all the nations shall flow to it,
>> and many peoples shall come, and say:
> 'Come, let us go up to the mountain of the LORD,
>> to the house of the God of Jacob;
> that he may teach us his ways
>> and that we may walk in his paths.'
> For out of Zion shall go forth the law
>> and the word of the LORD from Jerusalem.
> He shall judge between the nations...

In Messianic times ('in the end of the days') Jerusalem is here pictured as the religious centre of the world, whence God Himself will instruct people in His ways. Torah shall go forth from Zion and his word from Jerusalem. The 'instruction' or 'torah' of the future Jerusalem would be, we cannot doubt, in line with the Torah of Sinai.

## B. *The Apocrypha, Pseudepigrapha*

The material to be dealt with under this heading is confusing and the following classification is made only for convenience.

(1) *There are passages which connect the outpouring of wisdom with the ideal future or the Messianic Age.*

Judaism came to identify wisdom with the Law at an early date: they are already associated in Deut. iv. 6, which reads:

Keep them and do them; for that will be your wisdom and your understanding in the sight of the peoples, who, when they hear all these statutes, will say, 'Surely this great nation is a wise and understanding people.'

So it is a fair inference that a richer knowledge of the Law would be gained in the Messianic Age. The following are the pertinent passages.

We first turn to 1 Enoch. In a vision, which he calls a vision of wisdom, Enoch is granted to see that which is to come. To him is revealed the coming judgement of the wicked (xxxviii), the abode of the Elect One, who is marked by righteousness (xxxix); and later it is revealed to him that this Elect One or the Son of Man is very closely associated not only with righteousness but also with wisdom. Thus in xlviii. 1 we read:

> And in that place I saw the fountain of righteousness
> Which was inexhaustible:
> And around it were many fountains of wisdom:
> And all the thirsty drank of them,
> And they were filled with wisdom,
> And their dwellings were with the righteous and holy and
>     elect.
> And at that hour the Son of Man was named
> In the presence of the Lord of Spirits,
> And his name before the Head of Days.

Further on there is mention again of the power and wisdom of the Elect One who is to be the judge of the righteous and the wicked 'in those days' that are to come. Chapter xlix. 1 f. reads:

> For wisdom is poured out like water,
> And glory faileth not before him for evermore.
> For he is mighty in all the secrets of righteousness,
> And unrighteousness shall disappear as a shadow,
> And have no continuance...

And in li. 3 we read:

> And the Elect One shall in those days sit on My throne,
> And his mouth shall pour forth all the secrets of wisdom and
>     counsel:
> For the Lord of Spirits hath given (them) to him...

There is in the above probably a reference, under the figure of Wisdom, to the Torah. And we cannot doubt that for the author of the Similitudes the righteous are those who have been faithful to the Torah, and it is in accordance with the Torah, we can be sure, that the Elect One will judge (see xxxviii. 2, xxxix. 6, xlvi. 2, liii. 6). The association of the Elect One with wisdom may also be significant because from early times wisdom had been associated with Torah, as in Deut. iv. 6, and as early as Ecclesiasticus was actually identified with the Torah. The passage concerned from Ecclesiasticus is interesting; it reads (xxiv. 3 ff.):

> I came forth from the mouth of the Most High
> And as a mist I covered the earth...
> Alone I compassed the circuit of heaven,
> And in the depth of the abyss I walked.
> Over the waves of the sea, and over all the earth,
> And over every people and nation I held sway.
> With all these I sought a resting place
> And (said) In whose inheritance shall I lodge?
> Then the Creator of all things gave me commandment,
> And he that created me fixed my dwelling place (for me),
> And he said: Let thy dwelling place be in Jacob
> And in Israel take up thine inheritance.

In verse 23 the identification of Wisdom with the Torah is made explicit:

> All these things are the book of the Covenant of God Most High,
> The Law which Moses commanded (as) an heritage for the assemblies of Jacob.

Here Wisdom has found the completely satisfying home in the Torah on earth. Now, in 1 Enoch this view is not found. Instead we have a curious passage, which looks like an interpolation in its present context, where the view is expressed that Wisdom searched the earth in vain for a satisfactory home and failing to find such returned to heaven. The passage (1 Enoch xlii. 1 ff.) reads:

Wisdom found no place where she might dwell;
Then a dwelling place was assigned her in the heavens.
Wisdom went forth to make her dwelling among the children
    of men
And found no dwelling place:
Wisdom returned to her place,
And took her seat among the angels....

It agrees with this that there are several passages where it is claimed that Wisdom in its fullness is the mark of the Messianic existence, see xlviii. 1, xlix. 1 f., compare v. 8, xci. 10, 2 Bar. xliv. 14; Charles comments on Wisdom in xlii. 1 f. that 'she will return in Messianic times'; and with Wisdom, we may confidently repeat, goes the Torah in its fullness. The Son of Man, when he should come, would therefore be accompanied by or endowed with wisdom. But, while 1 Enoch would seem certainly to emphasize the character of this wisdom as knowledge of divine mysteries hidden since the creation and of the purpose of God for the world, we may assume that it also connoted knowledge of the Law, because the Son of Man was 'mighty in all the secrets of righteousness'.

## (2) *Certain persons are expected to interpret the Law in the future*

There are two passages in 1 Maccabees (written around 100 B.C.) which look forward to a coming prophet who would at some future time make plain certain difficulties which beset the interpretation of the Law in the present world. The first is in 1 Macc. iv. 41–6:

Then Judas appointed certain men to fight against those that were in the fortress, until he had cleansed the sanctuary. And he chose blameless priests, such as had delight in the Law; and they cleansed the Holy Place, and bare out the stones of defilement into an unclean place. And they took counsel concerning the altar of burnt offerings, which had been profaned, what they should do with it. And a good idea occurred to them (namely) to pull it down, lest it should be a reproach unto them because the Gentiles had defiled it; so they pulled down the altar and laid down the stones until a prophet should come and decide (as to what should be done) concerning them.

And in the second, 1 Macc. xiv. 25–49, the specific words which concern us are:

And the Jews and the priests were well pleased that Simon should be their leader and high priest for ever, until a faithful prophet should arise.

Both these passages refer difficulties in the interpretation of the Law to a coming prophet who should have a communication from God which would solve these. The reference to a coming prophet may be based on Deuteronomy xviii. 15, but nothing demands that 'the prophet' in these texts should be interpreted messianically. Nevertheless, they may be cited as confirming the view that the Law would at least be better understood in the future than in the present and that prophetic revelation of the meaning of the Law was part of the hope of Judaism.

## C. *The Dead Sea Scrolls (DSS) and The Zadokite Documents (CDC)*

Next we turn to the DSS and the CDC, the pre-Christian dating of which has been accepted by the majority of scholars. They reveal a group of people who, as they await the End, constitute themselves as the people of the New Covenant. Their activity seems to have been governed by the concept of a New Exodus parallel to the first. Their preoccupation with the Law of Moses shines clear. What we are here concerned to discover is whether they reveal an awareness of a need or hope for changes in the Law or for a New Law. The following passages are pertinent:

DSD ix. 9–11:

They shall not depart from any counsel of the Law, walking in all the stubbornness of their hearts; but they shall judge by the first judgements by which the men of the community began to be disciplined, until there shall come a prophet and the Messiahs of Aaron and Israel. (M. Burrows's translation.)

Thus the community, which, from DSD viii. 13–14, we know was formed on the basis of Isa. xl. 3, was to be governed by the rules laid down in the Manual until a prophet and 'Messiahs', one of Aaron and one of David, should arise. While there is nothing in the text to suggest that the prophet to come would bring a New Law, the very clear implication is that the rules governing the life of the community would be open to change on his coming. Thus the rules of the DSD constitute an interim programme.

The same concept of an interim programme emerges in CDC. In the opening of this document, in i. 10–12, after a statement about the original members of the community (who, though earnest in their ways, 'were like the blind and like them that grope *their* way' for twenty years) we read:

And God considered their works, for 'with a perfect heart' did they seek Him; | and He raised for them 'a teacher of righteousness' to lead them in 'the way of His heart' and to make known | to the last generations that which He ⌜would do⌝ to the last generation, the congregation of the faithless. (Rabin's translation.)

We are probably to understand that the instructions for 'the Way' given by this figure, the Teacher of Righteousness, are contained in CDC. Are these regarded as eternally binding? Words in CDC vi. 14 suggest that they were not. They constituted rather an interim ethic. Here the sectarians are to take care 'to do according to the exact statement of the Law for the epoch of wickedness'.

Beyond 'the epoch of wickedness' the present writ, it is implied, did not run.

But one thing is certain. In both DSD and CDC a future is envisaged in which a change in the laws governing the community is expected. The phraseology employed does not make it clear how the Law was conceived to operate in the Messianic Age: certainly we are not permitted to claim that at that time it would cease or that there would be a New Law, but only that the current interpretations would be obsolete. This means, however, that 'the Law' for the sect (whether we postulate the stages, as indicated above, or not) was not completely adequate. There was an intense awareness that the days of the Messiah would introduce changes in the laws governing the community.

Can we go further? There is one extended passage which suggests perhaps a radical break in the Messianic Age in DSD iv. 18–26. The pertinent words are in iv. 25:

For in equal measure God has established the two spirits until the period which has been decreed and *the making new*... (M. Burrows's translation.)

Is the 'making new', referred to in the above passage, to include the Law itself? This is a real possibility; because the Sect was aware of tension under the Law. The concentration, relentless and rigid, on obedience to the Law and the intense awareness of sin which accompanied this tension shine equally clear. In no other sources in first-century Judaism is failure to achieve the righteousness of the Law more recognized and at the same time its demands pressed with greater ruthlessness. May it be that this condition may have led to the hope that the Messianic Age would bring relief? This possibility is perhaps further to be discerned in the yearning expressed in the above passage for fullness of knowledge in the Messianic Age. The chief end of man is here defined in terms of the knowledge of God: it is to share in the wisdom of the angelic hosts. How is this knowledge to be understood? Is it more knowledge in and through the Law or is it knowledge beyond the Law? There is evidence that in the Scrolls the 'knowledge' which marks the final time is eschatological not only in the sense that it belongs to the final time but in the sense that it gives insight into the meaning of the events of that time. Should we go further and find among the Sectarians a yearning for a knowledge which itself constitutes 'eternal life', which transcends the knowledge supplied by the 'Law' as known in this present age? We can at least claim that Judaism is here straining at the leash of the Law: the Scrolls reveal it at 'boiling point'.

Notice that the agent of the new understanding of the Law which would be given in the ideal future would be a prophet, who accompanies the Messiah perhaps but is not himself Messianic. This is made clear in the passage from the DSD ix. 9–11, which we have already cited. We can be certain that the sectarians at Qumran expected the Messianic Age to remove the inadequacies of their understanding of the Law. While there is no suggestion that they anticipated any New Law (such is unlikely to be implicit in DSD iv. 18 ff.), in the 'making of the New' the Law itself was not to escape attention: it too required redemption, at least in its interpretation. And one eschatological figure, at least, the Prophet, as the New Moses, was to provide a new understanding of it.

Our survey of the Old Testament, the Apocrypha and Pseudepigrapha is now complete. When we ask what evidence it supplies for the role which the Torah would play in the Messianic Age, we can assert that that Age was expected to be a period when the rebelliousness of 'Israel' would be undone and righteousness enthroned. We have had no reason to believe that in most, if not in all cases, this righteousness would differ from that which was demanded by the Torah; and we may endorse the words of Moore as far as the Old Testament, the Apocrypha and Pseudepigrapha are concerned, at least that 'inasmuch as the days of the Messiah are the religious as well as the political consummation of the national history, and, however idealized, belong to the world we live in, it is natural that the law should not only be in force in the Messianic Age, but should be better studied and better observed than ever before; and this was indubitably the common belief'. Nevertheless, we have encountered noteworthy features of the Messianic hope as it touches upon our quest. The belief was obviously cherished that the Torah would be interpreted in a more satisfactory and glorious fashion and would also come to include the Gentiles in its sway. We failed to decide definitely whether Jeremiah's hope that there would be a new covenant implied a New Torah or whether it merely involved better obedience to the Old Torah, or again whether Jeremiah expected a condition of affairs in which no external Torah of any kind would be necessary. We suggested, however, that a certain tension between the written Torah and that Torah which would mark the New Covenant was probably not resolved by Jeremiah, although those who succeeded him appear to have understood his words as still referring to the Old Torah. It is clear, moreover, that the hope of a new covenant persisted as a dynamic element in Judaism as is witnessed by the Dead Sea Scrolls, where, especially, changes in the interpretation of the Law in the Messianic Age are anticipated, and it is well to remind ourselves again of the rich complex of concepts—covenantal,

Mosaic and Exodic—which informed the eschatological hope of Judaism, against which we make our way in this search.

## D. *The rabbinical sources*

When we turn to the rabbinical sources in our attempt to discover what role the Torah was expected to play in the Messianic Age, we must begin by recognizing certain commonplaces. First, it is always dangerous to impose any one mode of thought on Judaism: it could tolerate the widest varieties and even contradictions of beliefs. Moreover, it must be recognized that our rabbinic sources represent the triumph of only one stream within Judaism, the Pharisaic, and even of only one current within that one stream, that of R. Johannan ben Zakkai. Hence the possibility is to be reckoned with that many emphases or tendencies in Judaism in the first century are not represented in our rabbinic sources; and this is a possibility which, in view of the antagonism which arose between the Old Israel and its Torah and the New Israel with its new commandment, is not negligible in the present inquiry. Possibly much in the tradition about the nature and role of Torah in the Messianic Age has been either ignored or deliberately suppressed or modified. We have elsewhere emphasized the heterogeneity of first-century Judaism. This has been amply insisted upon in the works of Daube, Goodenough, Lieberman and Morton Smith, and it cannot be overlooked in this quest.

On the other hand, it has to be recognized also that, by the first century, that movement which received its greatest impulse from Ezra and which was designed to make Jewry a people of the Torah had come to fruition: Pharisaism had become well established even if its first-century significance has often been overemphasized. And for many

Jews the Torah had become the cornerstone of life. How true this was can be grasped not only from those episodes in Jewish history where loyalty to the Torah was the crucial factor governing religious activity in politics and other spheres, but also from the glorification of Torah in much Jewish thought. As Moore has made so clear, so central was the Torah for Judaism that it could conceive neither of the present nor of the past and future except in terms of Torah. The significance of the Torah in the present is demonstrated by that regulation of all life in its minutest details in accordance with the Torah which ultimately led to the codification of the Mishnah, a codification which was not a mushroom growth but the fruit of much previous codification which goes back at least to the first century. The significance of the Torah in the past was secured by the development of the belief that the Torah was not only pre-existent—as were certain other pivots of Jewish life—but also, and more vitally, instrumental in the creation of the world. The evidence for this need not be repeated here, because it is only with the Torah in the future that we are concerned, and the place of the Torah in the future was guaranteed by the development of the 'doctrine' which we know as that of the immutability of the Torah.    5:18

This 'doctrine' we may briefly characterize as follows. The Torah, whether written or oral, had been given to Moses by Yahweh. As the gift of Yahweh and as the ground plan of the Universe it could not but be perfect and unchangeable; it was impossible that it should ever be forgotten; no prophet could ever arise who would change it, and no new Moses should ever appear to introduce another Law to replace it. This was not only Palestinian belief but also that of Hellenistic Judaism. Philo, in a passage where he contrasts the unchanging Torah with the ever-changing laws of other nations, writes: 'The provisions of this law alone, stable, unmoved, unshaken, as it were stamped with the seal of nature itself, remain in fixity from the day they were written until now, and for the future we expect them to abide through all time as immortal, so long as the sun and moon and the whole heaven and the world exist.' Moore suggested that the association of the Torah with Wisdom helped in the development of this view. We are also tempted to find, as we shall point out later, that a certain polemic motive entered into the insistence on the 'doctrine'. But whatever be the contributory factors in its rise, and it is far too pronounced and early merely to be a polemic reaction against Christian teaching, we can be certain that the words in Matt. v. 18*a* adequately express what came to be the dominant 'doctrine' of rabbinic Judaism.

Thus the developed (rabbinic) Judaism revealed to us in our sources was not a soil in which the belief in any radical changes in the existing Torah was likely to grow or a soil which would welcome a new Torah. On the one hand, a preliminary consideration—the hospitable comprehensiveness of Judaism—should make us prepared for variety in the treatment of the Torah, while, on the other hand, another preliminary consideration—the dominance even in pre-Christian times of the 'doctrine' of the immutability of the Torah—should make us hesitate before accepting any other view too easily. With these two preliminaries recognized we can now proceed with our task. The following factors are relevant.

## (1) *The Role of Elijah at the End*

In Mal. iv. 5 we read:

'Behold, I will send you Elijah the prophet before the great and terrible day of the Lord comes. And he will turn the hearts of fathers to their children and the hearts of children to their fathers, lest I come and smite the land with a curse.'

Already in pre-Christian Judaism Elijah had become a figure of the End: while not strictly a Messianic figure himself, he was a Messianic forerunner. Under the Rabbis the figure of Elijah underwent a process of rabbinization so that in the rabbinic sources he appears as one who would explain points in the Torah which had baffled the Rabbis. Many passages attest this. One will suffice our purposes: it reveals not only that the significance of Elijah was a living issue in first-century Judaism but that possibly it was a living issue in its dialogue with Christianity. The passage is from Mishnah Eduyoth viii. 7 (H. Danby's translation of *The Mishnah*, p. 436). It reads:

R. Joshua said: I have received as a tradition from Rabban Johanan b. Zakkai, who heard from his teacher, and his teacher from his teacher, as a *Halakah* given to Moses from Sinai, that Elijah will not come to declare unclean or clean, to remove afar or to bring nigh, but to remove afar those [families] that were brought nigh by violence and to bring nigh those [families] that were removed afar by violence. The family of Beth Zerepha was in the land beyond Jordan and Ben Zion removed it afar by force. And yet another [family] was there, and Ben Zion brought it nigh by force. The like of these Elijah will come to declare unclean or clean, to remove afar or to bring nigh. R. Judah says: To bring nigh but not to remove afar. R. Simeon says: To bring agreement where there is matter for dispute. And the Sages say: Neither to remove afar nor to bring nigh, but to make peace in the world, as it is written, *Behold I will send you Elijah the prophet . . . and he shall turn the heart of the fathers to the children and the heart of the children to their fathers.*

Two tasks are assigned to Elijah by the various Rabbis mentioned in this passage. He is to pronounce on questions of legitimate Israelitish descent, that is, declare what is clean and unclean, and to create peace. Elijah would be the instrument of changes in the understanding of the Law in Messianic times.

## (2) *Modifications to be made to the Torah*

Our sources do reveal an awareness that, even though the Torah was immutable, nevertheless modifications of

various kinds, at least in certain details, would be necessary. We shall group the material as follows:

(a) *Passages suggesting the cessation of certain enactments
concerning festivals, etc.* There were some who held the view
that in the Messianic Age sin would not exist, and it
followed that the vast majority of sacrifices, which
naturally dealt with the taint of sin, would be irrelevant.
A passage in Leviticus Rabbah ix. 7 reads:

R. Phinehas and R. Levi and R. Johanan said in the name of
R. Menahem of Gallia: In the time to come all sacrifices will be
annulled, but that of thanksgiving will not be annulled, and all
prayers will be annulled, but [that of] thanksgiving will not be
annulled. This is [indicated by] what is written: Jer. xxxiii. 11.
(Soncino translation.)

The phrase 'In the time to come' here probably refers to the
Messianic Age and the date of the passage is A.D. 165–200.

A passage from Yalqut on Prov. ix. 2, which dates from
about A.D. 80–120, reads as follows:

All the festivals will cease but not Purim since it is said (Esther ix. 28)
'...these days shall be...throughout every generation...and...
should not fail from among the Jews...' R. Eleazar said: The Day of
Atonement too will not cease since it is said (Lev. xvi. 34) 'And this
shall be unto you an everlasting statute'.

Here the two festivals of Purim and the Day of Atonement
alone among the festivals are to survive into the Messianic
Age. This implies that radical changes in the festivals in
that Age were contemplated.

(b) *Passages which seem to suggest changes in the laws concerning things clean and unclean, etc.* We begin with a passage
from Midrash Tehillim on Ps. cxlvi. 7. This is translated
by Braude as follows:

*The Lord will loose the bonds* (Ps. cxlvi. 7). What does the verse mean
by the words *loose the bonds*? Some say that of every animal whose
flesh it is forbidden to eat in this world, the Holy One, blessed be He,
will declare in the time-to-come that the eating of its flesh is per-

mitted. Thus in the verse *That which hath been is that which shall be, and that which hath been given is that which shall be given* (Eccles. i. 9), the words *that which hath been given* refer to the animals that were given as food before the time of the sons of Noah, for God said: 'Every moving thing that liveth shall be food for you; as the green herb have I given you all' (Gen. ix. 3). That is to say, 'As I give the green herb as food to all, so once I gave both beasts and cattle as food to all'. But why did God declare the flesh of some animals forbidden? In order to see who would accept His commandments and who would not accept them. In the time-to-come, however, God will again permit the eating of that flesh which He has forbidden.

Others say that in the time-to-come, God will not permit this, for it is said *They that...eat swine's flesh, and the detestable thing, and the mouse, shall be consumed together, saith the Lord* (Isa. lxvi. 17). Now if God will cut off and destroy men who eat forbidden flesh, surely he will do the same to the forbidden animals themselves. To what, otherwise, do the words *will loose the bonds* refer? Though nothing is more strongly forbidden than intercourse with a menstruous woman—for when a woman sees blood the Holy One, blessed be He, forbids her to her husband—in the time-to-come, God will permit such intercourse. As Scripture says, *It shall come to pass in that day, saith the Lord of hosts, that...I will cause the prophets and the unclean spirit to pass out of the land* (Zech. xiii. 2), the *unclean* clearly denoting a menstruous woman, and of such it is said '*And thou shalt not approach a woman to uncover her nakedness, as long as she is impure by her uncleanness*' (Lev. xviii. 19).

Still others say that in the time-to-come sexual intercourse will be entirely forbidden. You can see for yourself why it will be. On the day that the Holy One, blessed be He, revealed Himself on Mount Sinai to give the Torah to the children of Israel, He forbade intercourse for three days, as it is said *Be ready against the third day; come not at your wives* (Exod. xix. 15). Now since God, when He revealed Himself for only one day, forbade intercourse for three days, in the time-to-come, when the presence of God dwells continuously in Israel's midst, will not intercourse be entirely forbidden?

What, otherwise, is meant by *bonds* in *will loose the bonds*? The bonds of death and the bonds of the netherworld.

Here distinctions between clean and unclean animals are to be abrogated in the Messianic Age, which is pictured as a return to the primitive or original condition of the world before the disaster of the flood: the idea that the End corresponds to the Beginning is a commonplace of apocalyptic and the principle would seem to be operative here. What concerns us, however, is that the text suggests the possibility of change in the Law in the future. Unfortunately the date of this passage is unknown.

This is the best place also to quote a passage which we may almost certainly understand to imply the coming of a New Torah in the Messianic Age. The passage from Leviticus Rabbah xiii. 3 reads as follows:

R. Judan b. R. Simeon said: Behemoth and the Leviathan are to engage in a wild beast contest before the righteous in the Time to Come, and whoever has not been a spectator at the wild beast contests of the heathen nations in this world will be accorded the boon of seeing one in the World to Come. How will they be slaughtered? Behemoth will, with its horns, pull Leviathan down and rend it, and Leviathan will, with its fins, pull Behemoth down and pierce it through. The Sages said: And is this a valid method of slaughter? Have we not learnt the following in a Mishnah: All may slaughter, and one may slaughter at all times (of the day), and with any instrument except with a scythe, or with a saw, or with teeth (in a jaw cut out of a dead animal), because they cause pain as if by choking, or with a nail (of a living body)? R. Abin b. Kahana said: The Holy One, blessed be He, said: Instruction [Torah] shall go forth from Me (Isa. li. 4) [that is, an exceptional temporary ruling will go forth from me]. (Israelstam's Soncino translation.)

The above translation by Israelstam ignores the text of the Wilna and Warsaw editions of the Midrash which demands the translation: 'New Torah shall go forth from Me.' Many have held that here the concept of a New Messianic Torah is explicit. The date of R. Abin b. Kahana is probably at least as late as A.D. 300.

The evidence presented above sufficiently justifies the claim that despite the 'doctrine' of the immutability of Torah, there were also occasional expressions of expectations that Torah would suffer modification in the Messianic Age. There were some Halakoth which would cease to be applicable in that age; others, by contrast, would acquire a new relevance. It is important, however, to recognize explicitly that most, if not all, the changes envisaged were deemed to occur within the context of the existing Torah and presuppose the continuance of its validity. Moreover, the changes contemplated imply no necessary diminution in what we may be allowed to term the severity of the yoke of the Torah. On the contrary, that yoke, in some passages, was expected to become even heavier than in this age (see especially Midrash Tehillim cxlvi. 7). In addition we have to point out that much of the traditional Christian interpretation of some of the passages cited does violence to the text and has to be rejected. It may also be helpful to state at this point that in all the passages so far quoted the reference probably is to the Messianic Age as such.

## (3) *The Torah to be fully comprehended*

The third significant factor which we have to notice is that the Messianic Age, as indeed we might expect, is described as an era in which certain difficulties or incomprehensibilities which the Torah presented in this age would be adequately explained and comprehended: now we see in a glass darkly, but then obscurities will be removed.

Many of the demands of the Torah seemed inexplicable and irrational: the reasons why certain things had been forbidden or commanded were obscure, and the fact that Jewry could not always give a satisfying apology for much in their practice laid them open to the attacks of Gentile cynicism and criticism. Hence there necessarily developed a considerable activity in the Tannaitic period, and earlier probably, in an attempt to explain why certain things had been commanded which at first seemed even merely stupid. So eager were some to explain 'the grounds or reasons for the Torah's demands', that they were in danger of manipulating their texts, and consequently incurred suspicion. The normative position arrived at was that in this world the demands of Torah were to be obeyed because they were commanded: this was sufficient reason for their observance. This is made clear in the words of R. Johanan b. Zakkai (we quote the passage from Numbers Rabbah xix. 8 on xix. 2 because it illustrates the kind of criticism which was made of the demands of the Torah):

An idolater asked R. Johanan b. Zakkai: These rites that you perform look like a kind of witchcraft. You bring a heifer, burn it, pound it, and take its ashes. If one of you is defiled by a dead body you sprinkle upon him two or three drops and you say to him: 'Thou art clean.' R. Johanan asked him: 'Has the demon of madness ever possessed you?' 'No!' he replied. 'Have you ever seen a man entered by this demon of madness?' 'Yes,' said he. 'And what do you do in such a case?' 'We bring roots,' he replied, 'and make them smoke under him, then we sprinkle water upon the demon and it flees.' Said R. Johanan to him: 'Let your ears hear what you utter with your mouth: Precisely so is this spirit a spirit of uncleanness: as it is written, *And also I will cause the prophets and the unclean spirit to pass out of the land* (Zech. xiii. 2). Water of purification is sprinkled upon the unclean and the spirit flees.' When the idolater had gone R. Johanan's disciples said to their master: 'Master!' This man you have put off with a mere makeshift but what explanation will you give to us?' Said he to them: 'By your life! It is not the dead that defiles nor the water that purifies! The Holy One, blessed be He, merely says: "I have laid down a statute, I have issued a decree. You are not allowed to transgress My decree"; as it is written, *This is the statute of the law*' (Num. xix. 2).

But although theirs was not to reason why in this world, the Rabbis were convinced that the Messianic Age would bring with it an explanation of the inexplicable demands that the Torah made in this world. We have previously quoted passages from the Old Testament where the

Messianic Age was depicted as a time when God himself would teach his people. This was the firm conviction of the rabbis also. In illustration we shall again quote a passage from Numbers Rabbah xix. 6 on xix. 2, despite its later date, where the reference is not strictly to the Messianic Age, however, but to the final Age to Come:

THAT THEY BRING THEE A RED HEIFER (xix. 2). R. Jose b. Hanina (the second half of the third century) expounded: The Holy One, blessed be He, said to Moses: 'To thee I shall disclose the reason for the Heifer, but to anybody else it is a statute.' For R. Huna said: It is written, *When I* take the appointed time [i.e. in the World to Come], *I Myself will judge with equity* (Ps. lxxv. 3) [i.e. reveal the reasons for My Laws], and it is also written, *And it shall come to pass in that day, that there shall not be light, but heavy clouds and thick*—wekippa'on (Zech. xiv. 6). The written form is 'yekippa'on', as much as to say: The things that are concealed from you in this world, you will see in the World to Come, like a blind man who regains his sight, as it is written (Isa. xlii. 16), *And I will bring the blind by a way that they know not...* (Soncino translation, Numbers, vol. II, 756).

We pass on to the next group of material.

## (4) *A New Torah envisaged*

Despite the changes both in the substance and interpretation of the Torah which they contemplate, those passages which we have so far examined have afforded little if any evidence for the expectation of a New Torah in the Messianic Age. Changes in details and an increase in understanding there would be, but no substitution of the old Torah by a new one was envisaged. In this section we must deal with passages where it has been claimed that it is possible that a New Torah is expressly indicated.

(*a*) *The Targum on Isa.* xii. 3, 'And you shall draw water in joy from the wells of salvation'. The whole context of the passage is Messianic: xii. 1–3 reads in its entirety:

1  You will say in that day:
   'I will give thanks to thee, O LORD,
     for though thou wast angry with me,
   thy anger turned away,
     and thou didst comfort me.
2  'Behold, God is my salvation;
     I will trust, and will not be afraid;
   for the LORD GOD is my strength and my song,
     and he has become my salvation.'
3  With joy you will draw water from the wells of salvation.

xii. 3 is rendered by the Targum: 'And ye shall receive new instruction with joy from the chosen of righteousness', but the term translated 'new instruction' here may well mean 'new Torah'. The date of the Targum is about 200 A.D.

(b) In Yalqut on Isa. xxvi. 2 there is an explicit reference to a New Messianic Torah designed not only for Israel but for all the nations. But since the pertinent passage is probably to be dated in the thirteenth century A.D. it is too late to be of use here. We need only note here that there are other earlier passages which refer to the participation of the Gentiles in the blessings of the Torah in the Messianic Age.

There were different views as to what demands would be made on the Gentiles: according to some all the minute details of the Torah would be imposed upon them: according to others only three ordinances would be binding upon them: according to still others the Noachian commandments would be placed upon them. We need not here enlarge on the details: it is the fact that is significant: that in the opinion of some rabbis at least the Gentiles would submit to the yoke of the Torah in the Messianic Age.

(5) *An Age without Torah*

Next we have to ask whether there are passages which have been held to suggest, not merely that there would be changes in the Torah in the Messianic Age, but that it would be completely abrogated.

The chief passage to be considered comes from the Babylonian Talmud Sanhedrin 97 *a* (the end) and Abodah Zarah 9 *a* (middle). The Soncino translation of the former is:

*The Tanna debe Eliyyahu* taught: The world is to exist six thousand years. In the first two thousand years there was desolation; two thousand years the Torah flourished; and the next two thousand years is the Messianic era [97 b] but through our many iniquities all these years have been lost.

This probably comes from the period before A.D. 200. Some have argued that this passage implies that a Messianic era without Torah is set over against this present era. But the passages usually appealed to in support of this view are not altogether convincing. The passage may merely mean that this Age is to be set over against the Messianic Age, not that the latter is to be without Torah.

In the passages treated above we have sought to discover what part the Torah was expected to play in the ideal future, whether conceived as a Messianic Age or as the ultimate Age to Come. To recapitulate, we found in the Old Testament, the Apocrypha and Pseudepigrapha and in the rabbinical sources the profound conviction that obedience to the Torah would be a dominating mark of the Messianic Age, and in the prophet Jeremiah a certain tension as to whether this obedience would be spontaneous, in the sense that it would not be directed to, nor governed by, any external code, or whether some form of external Torah would still be operative. Generally, however, our sources revealed the expectation that the Torah in its existing form would persist into the Messianic Age, when its obscurities would be made plain, and when there would be certain natural adaptations and changes and, according to some, the inclusion of the Gentiles among those who accepted the yoke of the Torah. The most conscious and general recognition of the need for legal changes in the Messianic Age emerged in the DSS.

The evidence for the expectation of a New Torah which the Messiah should bring was not sufficiently definite and unambiguous to make us certain that this was a well defined and accepted element in the Messianic hope, but neither was it inconsiderable and questionable enough for us to dismiss it as merely a late development in a Judaism influenced by Christianity, a point to which we shall return later. We can at least affirm that there were elements inchoate in the Messianic hope of Judaism, which could make it possible for some to regard the Messianic Age as marked by a New Torah, new, indeed, not in the sense that it contravened the old, and yet not merely in the sense that it affirmed the old on a new level, but in such a way as to justify the adjective "new" that was applied to it. (Possibly Jeremiah would have thought of a Torah new in kind, but even he, as we suggested, did not exclude the possibility of this new kind of Torah having at the same time an external element in it like that of the Old Torah.)

Certain difficulties have to be noted which touch the passages which deal with a New Torah. They are post-Christian and late. This means that only with extreme caution can they be applied to the New Testament. They are also *haggadic* in character, that is, homiletic: they do not belong to the *halakic*, that is, the strictly legal sources of Judaism. This means, according to most rabbinic authorities, that they are not to be taken as theologically serious but merely as playful fancy. But to offset these two difficulties certain considerations are important.

First, we must emphasize that the silence of our sources as to an early belief in a New Torah may be due to deliberate surgery. As Christians came to emphasize the demand of Jesus as a New Teaching or as the Law of the Messiah, Judaism deliberately avoided such concepts. There is a parallel to this in the fact that as Christianity more and more understood the New Covenant, the idea of the Covenant became less and less exploited in rabbinical circles.

Secondly, there are rabbinic scholars who insist that Haggadah (homiletic material), not only Halakah (legal material), is theologically serious.

At this point we must return to the *SM*.

The material presented above is sufficiently cogent to illumine for us the Matthaean understanding of the *SM*. Matthew was conscious, as were other early Christians, of living in the Messianic Age: the role of the Law, therefore, inevitably occupied him. We saw that for him the Christian Dispensation, among other things, denies the Old Law on one level, but affirms and fulfils it on another; this is the meaning of the *SM*. Matthew does not explicitly claim to have received a *New* Torah, although the substance of a New Messianic Torah is clearly present to his mind. As the Rabbis, and especially the Dead Sea Sectarians, anticipated, the Messianic Age had brought for Matthew a teaching with eschatological authority. In his emphasis on the Messianic teaching in the *SM*, Matthew reveals especial affinity, perhaps, with the Sectarians, who had very unequivocally contrasted the 'judgements' by which they were to be ruled after the Prophet and the Messiahs of Aaron and Israel had come, with the interim ones to which, until then, they were subject. But, unless the Messiah of Aaron be equated with Elias *redivivus*, which is unlikely, the Sectarians had ascribed the giving of these anticipated new judgements to the Prophet, that is, the Messianic function was not strictly connected with the promulgation of new laws. In connecting Jesus, as Messiah, especially with the giving of teaching, Matthew differs from the Sectarians: that is, the teaching in the *SM* is more specifically that of the Messiah in Matthew's view, than would have been the case had the Sectarians found that their Messiahs had come. In his awareness of the significance of the moral teaching of Jesus, as belonging to the Messianic Age, Matthew has Sectarian affinities, but in pinning this down to Jesus as *the Messiah himself* he departs from the sectarian anticipation.

Does he, at this very point, attach himself to the rabbinic anticipation? The passages to which we have appealed justify the view that in some rabbinic circles the Messiah had a didactic function. And it is this emphasis that Matthew found congenial. His is, in this sense, in part a rabbinic Christ, whose words were for him *halakah* and the ground for *halakah* both for Israel and for the Gentile world: both Israel and the latter are addressed in these words of Jesus. At this point again it is impossible to claim Matthew for any single milieu; he reveals both sectarian and rabbinic affinities. One thing is clear: even if the concept of a New Torah in the Messianic Age had not become explicit in Judaism before Christ (which is not at all sure), his figure was a catalyst which gave life to what was inchoate: with him came also a 'law of the Messiah'.

But despite his sense of the didactic significance of Jesus the Messiah, Matthew nevertheless remains sensitive to the niceties of the expectations of Judaism. It was this sensitivity, in part at least, that may have made him hesitate to use the phrase 'new teaching' or 'new Law of the Messiah'. The ambiguity of Jewish expectation has invaded the Evangelist's presentation of the Messianic era. Nevertheless, the phrase 'New Torah' did emerge in Judaism and *may* have already emerged in the first century within Pharisaic Judaism; Paul did not hesitate to speak of 'the Law of Christ' and John of 'the New Commandment'. It is, therefore, probable that it was not only his sensitivity to the niceties of rabbinic and sectarian eschatological anticipations that caused Matthew to change the 'new teaching' of Mark i. 27 to the 'teaching' of vii. 27. There must have been other factors in his world which caused him to temper his language in this way. These we shall explore in the next chapter.

## Note

The attempt by Norman Perrin in his work entitled *The Kingdom of God in the Teaching of Jesus* (Westminster Press, Philadelphia, 1963, pp. 76–8) to prove that there prevailed in the Dead Sea Sect the expectation of a New Torah must be rejected. He is only able to hold such a view by what is, in my judgement, a mistranslation of one of the Liturgical Prayers printed on page 154 of *Discoveries in the Judaean Desert. 1; Qumran Cave I*, by D. Barthélemy, O. P., and J. T. Milik (Oxford, 1955). The passage is designated 1 Q 34. Perrin translates 1 Q 34 ii 2:5–8 as follows:

> In the time of thy good pleasure thou wilt choose for thyself a people, for thou hast remembered thy covenant and thou wilt make them to be set apart unto thee as holy and distinct from all the peoples, and thou wilt renew thy covenant unto them with a show of glory and with words of thy holy spirit, with works of thy hand and a writing of thy right hand to reveal to them the instructions of glory and the heights of eternity...for them a faithful shepherd.

But the Hebrew does not support such a translation. Apart from the dubiety of interpreting the phrase 'In the time of thy good pleasure' of the End-time (p. 77, n. 4), the verbs which Perrin renders as futures, in fact refer to the past. I accept the following rendering of the whole fragment by Millar Burrows in *More Light on the Dead Sea Scrolls* (Viking Press, New York, 1958, p. 399).

> But thou didst choose for thyself a people in the time of thy good pleasure; for thou rememberedst thy covenant. Thou didst...

them, separating them for thyself as holy from all the peoples; and thou didst renew thy covenant for them in a vision of glory and the words of thy holy Spirit with the works of thy hands and the writing of thy right hand, to make them know the discipline of glory and the ascents of eternity...to them a faithful shepherd... meek...

There is no ground here for Perrin's claim that the Scrolls present us with the expectation of a New Law.

# 3

# THE SETTING IN THE CONTEMPORARY JUDAISM

In one of his plays dealing with complex domestic issues, T. S. Eliot asserts that to understand any situation we must know its total setting:

SITZ

> It is often the case [says O'Reilly, the psychiatrist]
>     that my patients
> Are only pieces of a total situation
> Which I have to explore.

This is also true of any document we have to study and it is especially true of the documents of the NT—because these last were created to serve the needs of a community, and of a community, the Church, not enclosed within itself but ever concerned to present its faith to the world. Hence recent scholarship has rightly insisted that the various elements in the NT must be placed over against their 'setting in life'. This term, 'the setting in life', can be conceived in a narrow or a broad sense. In the narrow sense, 'the setting in life' of any document in the NT is its foreground in the life of the Church or Churches within which it emerged, its worship, catechesis, peculiar needs and circumstances. In the broad sense, 'the setting in life' has reference to the total environment of a document, to the whole range of circumstances, ecclesiastical, ideological, social and political under the pressure of which it came into being: in other words, to the fullness of its background in the contemporary world.

This holds true of Matthew. Its foreground, you will allow me to assume, is the life of the Church in Syria or Palestine somewhere between A.D. 75 and 100: its background the total circumstances of that period. Since I cannot here deal with the Gospel as a whole I shall concentrate on a significant part of it, the Sermon on the Mount. What were the influences which led to the elevation of the *SM* to its dominating position in the second edition of Mark which we call Matthew? What forces necessitated this concentrated and architectonic presentation of the moral demands of the Gospel?

*Salvage only 7:22*

## A. *Gnosticism*

First there is the possibility that 'Gnosticism' was a factor to be reckoned with in the presentation of the Gospel in Matthew's particular environment, and we shall now examine the claims made for the presence in Matthew of anti-Gnostic motifs. But before we can do so we shall have to indicate what is meant by Gnosticism. The term is usual in British and American scholarship to denote aberrant Christian movements of the second century and later. Since Matthew was written in the first century probably, Gnosticism in this sense cannot have had any influence on Matthew. But, secondly, Gnosticism has a wider meaning. Particularly in German and European scholarship, it is used to refer to a widespread movement which was pre-Christian and which had even influenced Judaism before the time of Jesus. This movement, as its name implies, emphasized 'knowledge', *gnôsis*, as a means to salvation. But 'knowledge' of what? Mainly, the knowledge that 'saved' consisted of knowledge about man's origin and man's destiny or fate: about the origin and nature of evil and of the way of escape from it. The myths in which the Gnostics indulged recount with manifold variations the fate of the soul. The soul has its origin in the world of light above; but its tragic fate was to fall from this upper world of light into the sphere of this earth:

it thus became an alien imprisoned in the body. But because God takes pity on the soul in its lostness in this world he sends down his heavenly son to redeem the soul and thus a return is made possible to the world of light. The Gnostic myth took a variety of forms, and it is not clear that all that is often included under Gnosticism should be so described. But accepting for the moment the largely Continental understanding of Gnosticism as pre-Christian, what we have to note is that there were emphases in it which often led to grave moral laxity. The Gnostic was tempted to believe that the knowledge which he possessed made him superior to the world. And this superiority could express itself in two opposite ways, either in an indifference to the world which led to moral licence, the abuse of the flesh, or in a contempt for the world which led to false asceticism. The lack of moral earnestness in Gnosticism and its seriousness for Christianity are pictured for us in the Book of Acts where the sorcerer Simon, who is regarded by the Church Fathers as the fountain-head of Gnosticism, offers to purchase the power of the Holy Spirit for money. Here is the story (Acts viii. 5 ff.):

Philip went down to a city of Samaria and proclaimed to them the Christ. And the multitudes with one accord gave heed to what was said by Philip, when they heard him and saw the signs which he did. For unclean spirits came out of many who were possessed, crying with a loud voice; and many who were paralyzed or lame were healed. So there was much joy in that city.

But there was a man named Simon who had previously practiced magic in the city and amazed the nation of Samaria, saying that he himself was somebody great. They all gave heed to him, from the least to the greatest, saying, 'This man is that power of God which is called Great.' And they gave heed to him, because for a long time he had amazed them with his magic. But when they believed Philip as he preached good news about the kingdom of God and the name of Jesus Christ, they were baptized, both men and women. Even Simon himself believed, and after being baptized he continued with Philip. And seeing signs and great miracles performed, he was amazed.

Now when the apostles at Jerusalem heard that Samaria had received the word of God, they sent to them Peter and John, who came down and prayed for them that they might receive the Holy Spirit; for it had not yet fallen on any of them, but they had only been baptized in the name of the Lord Jesus. Then they laid their hands on them and they received the Holy Spirit. Now when Simon saw that the Spirit was given through the laying on of the apostles' hands, he offered them money, saying, 'Give me also this power, that any one on whom I lay my hands may receive the Holy Spirit.' But Peter said to him, 'Your silver perish with you, because you thought you could obtain the gift of God with money! You have neither part nor lot in this matter, for your heart is not right before God. Repent therefore of this wickedness of yours, and pray to the Lord that, if possible, the intent of your heart may be forgiven you. For I see that you are in the gall of bitterness and in the bond of iniquity.' And Simon answered, 'Pray for me to the Lord, that nothing of what you have said may come upon me.'

There can be no doubt that the author of Acts here uses Simon as a symbol of the Gnostic challenge to the Church. Gnosticism signified the substitution of esoteric *gnôsis* for moral earnestness. Doubtless there were Gnostics of a high moral achievement. On the whole, however, they sacrificed morality to speculative or, better, visionary truth, and thus came to constitute a menace to the Church.

And the claim has been made that, when Matthew was preparing his Gospel, the Gnostic movement had become a serious threat to the Church: by proclaiming that 'knowledge', not obedience to God's will, was the means to salvation, it had led to grave moral laxity. And it was the necessity to combat this movement, it has been urged, that caused Matthew to emphasize the moral demands of the Gospel. The Sermon on the Mount is the protest of Matthew and his Church against the substitution of speculation, ecstasy and esoteric knowledge for morality. Let us now examine the evidence for this anti-Gnostic view of Matthew.

First, our attention is drawn to the birth narratives in

Matt. i and ii. In the Gospel of Mark there is no account of the birth of Jesus. From the first, Jesus is there presented as a full-grown man, who came to be baptized of John in Jordan: his birth, childhood, youth and early manhood are not mentioned. And some early Christians thought that this omission in Mark was highly significant. In fact, it could be claimed that Mark, by this omission, helped to prove that Jesus was not really a man at all; He only seemed to be such. Thus, the Gospel of Mark became a weapon for Christians who despised the flesh and refused to ascribe any fleshly reality to Jesus. These Christians came to be known as *docetists*, but they are closely allied to the Gnostics. Under their impact it became necessary for the Church to insist on the reality of the birth of Jesus. And it did so in the Gospel of Matthew, which is a revised version of Mark. The birth narratives, which insist on the human birth of Jesus, are designed, on this view, to counteract Gnostic asceticism and docetism. This was the view of B. W. Bacon. He referred by way of illustration to the Docetist Cerinthus (Gnostic heretic, *circa* A.D. 100) who, according to a Church Father, Irenaeus, (Bishop of Lyons, *c*. 130–*c*. 200) rested his view that Jesus only appeared to be a man solely on the Gospel of Mark. But the passages in Irenaeus dealing with Cerinthus make no explicit references to Mark. The opinions of Cerinthus are declared to be similar to those held by the Jewish Christians (the Ebionites) and they are stated to use only the Gospel of Matthew. More-over, it must be affirmed that the story of the birth of Jesus in Matthew itself may have led to doubts about the real manhood of Jesus, since he was said to have been born of the Spirit. The birth narrative in Matthew is not the kind of story which would have been inserted in a Gospel designed to combat Gnosticism. And, in any case, the Docetist Cerinthus is to be connected with Ephesus, not with Syria or Palestine. The view that the purpose of the birth stories in Matthew is anti-Gnostic cannot, therefore, be substantiated.

But, again, it has been urged that the very many references to false Christs and false teachers in Matthew are aimed at teachers of Gnosticism. Note the following:

(a) Matt. vii. 5:

Beware of false prophets, who come to you in sheep's clothing but inwardly are ravenous wolves. You will know them by their fruits.

Here undoubtedly we meet false *Christian* prophets. But there is no justification for pinning down this very general reference to Gnostics as such. No objection to pretensions to knowledge is explicitly made.

(b) Matt. xxiv. 11, 24:

xxiv. 11:

And many false prophets will arise and lead many astray.

xxiv. 24:

For false Christs and false prophets will arise and show great signs and wonders, so as to lead astray, if possible, even the elect.

Matthew is combatting false teachers and Christs within his Church but again the references are too vague to pin these down precisely to Gnosticism.

(c) Matt. xxiv. 5:

For many will come in my name, saying, 'I am the Christ,' and they will lead many astray.

This is a most important passage. Attempts have been made to connect this saying with Simon Magus, the father of Gnosticism about whom we have already spoken. But Simon Magus did not claim that he was 'the Christ' nor does he make any claim to come in the Name of Christ. Had Matthew been concerned with such a specific person as Simon in xxiv. 5, the reference would have been more explicit. So again we must conclude that the references to false prophets and false Christs in Matthew are not such as to allow us to identify them with Gnostics.

But the claim has further been made that the references to 'lawlessness' in Matthew are anti-Gnostic: he is combating the immorality and amorality of the Gnostics themselves. The term occurs in the following passages:

vii. 22 ff.: 7:22

On that day many will say to me, 'Lord, Lord, did we not prophesy in your name, and cast out demons in your name, and do many mighty works in your name?' And then will I declare to them, 'I never knew you; depart from me, you evildoers' [workers of lawlessness].

The people condemned here are false prophets who prophesied, cast out demons, performed miracles in the name of Christ. Nevertheless, they are workers of lawlessness. It is made clear that they are lawless because they have failed to do the will of God, that is, to obey the demands of the Father revealed by Jesus. The problem emerging here is clear. It is the discrepancy between the lives and the pretensions of those who preach and teach the Gospel *NB* but do not exhibit its fruits. It can be illustrated from the life of Paul. At the close of a passage dealing with his work as a preacher of the Gospel, Paul recognized that it was possible for him to preach to others and yet himself be found wanting. And this dread possibility, which re-echoes the warnings of Matt. vii. 15 ff., spurs the Apostle on to greater efforts in self-discipline:

I Cor. ix. 27:

But I pommel my body and subdue it, lest after preaching to others I myself should be disqualified.

Similarly the interest shown in the NT in the denials of Peter and in the inconsistencies of his career, point to the same concern in the Church. From the first, the Church was aware of the discrepancy between the *essential* nature of those who *outwardly* performed Christian service in preaching, exorcism, miracles and the faith they professed. They were often like rotten fruit. After all, how could a vacillating Peter lead the Church or be its Rock? This problem of the integrity of the leadership of the Church became extremely acute with the emergence of Gnosticism, but it marked the more orthodox life of the Church also. It emerged at a very early date in the Pauline and Palestinian Churches, so that there is no need to call in the menace of Gnosticism to account for it. Moreover, here again we note the absence of any reference in Matthew to the knowledge that puffeth up.

The other passages dealing with lawlessness are:

xiii. 41:

The Son of Man will send his angels, and they will gather out of his kingdom all causes of sin and all evildoers [workers of lawlessness].

xxiv. 12:

And because wickedness is multiplied, most men's love will grow cold.

xxiii. 28:

Even so ye also outwardly appear righteous unto men, but within ye are full of hypocrisy and lawlessness.

In all these passages there is no obvious reference to Gnostics. The term 'lawlessness' signifies, for Matthew, sin, because sin for him is the breaking of law, not the Jewish law, but the law which is God's will revealed in the words of Jesus. Matthew recognized a kind of Christian law of love, which constituted God's will. Inner and outward disobedience to this is lawlessness and unrighteousness. But there is no indication that he was thereby combating any specifically Gnostic denial of all legal restraint. Failure to obey the true will of God was lawlessness for Matthew among Scribes and Pharisees and in the Church, as elsewhere, and such failure in the Church, which meant the decline of love, he interpreted as a sign of the end of the world.

So far, then, it seems that neither the birth narratives nor the references to false teachers and to lawlessness suggest that Matthew is necessarily and particularly opposing Gnosticism. But other possibilities that this was in fact the case have been put forward.

First, there is the story of the temptation in iv. 3–11.   *4:3-11*

And the tempter came and said to him, 'If you are the Son of God, command these stones to become loaves of bread.' But he answered, 'It is written, "Man shall not live by bread alone, but by every word that proceeds from the mouth of God."' Then the devil took him to the holy city, and set him on the pinnacle of the temple, and said to him, 'If you are the Son of God, throw yourself down; for it is written, "He will give his angels charge of you," and "On their hands they will bear you up, lest you strike your foot against a stone."' Jesus said to him, 'Again it is written, "You shall not tempt the Lord your God."' Again, the devil took him to a very high mountain, and showed him all the kingdoms of the world and the glory of them; and he said to him, 'All these I will give you, if you will fall down and worship me.' Then Jesus said to him, 'Begone, Satan! for it is written, "You shall worship the Lord your God and him only shall you serve."' Then the devil left him, and behold, angels came and ministered to him.

What is the meaning of the temptation narrative? A German scholar, Schlatter, thought that its purpose was to contrast the Redeemer of Christians with the Redeemers of the Gnostics. The Redeemer of Christians, Jesus Christ, had to undergo conflict within himself, face the temptation to evil in his own will. In this he differed from the Gnostic Redeemers, who had to go through elaborate mythological conflicts with Satan and Evil. But this interpretation of the Temptation cannot be accepted on two grounds. First, there *is* a mythological element in the story of the temptation of Jesus. The early Fathers of the Church found in it the counterpart of the story of Adam, Christ being the second Adam, who did not succumb to temptation. If Matthew were consciously trying to avoid mythology at this point, he would have avoided any possibility of such an interpretation. But, secondly, this apart, the Temptation narrative in Matthew is governed very largely by reference to Deut. viii. Its aim is partly to show how the experience of the people of God under the Old Covenant is re-enacted in that of Jesus: Jesus himself relives the history of his own people and thus becomes in himself the people of God, and the inaugurator of a new covenant. Along with this the narrative aims, not at the rejection of Gnosticism so much as at that of the traditional Jewish Messianism. The main motif behind the Temptation narrative is the necessity of enlightening the disciples on the nature of the Messiahship of Jesus and the methods appropriate to such a Messiahship.

But there are two other important passages where anti-Gnosticism, it is claimed, breaks through in Matthew. First in the resurrection scene described in xxviii. 16 ff.

Now the eleven disciples went to Galilee, to the mountain to which Jesus had directed them. And when they saw him they worshipped him; but some doubted. And Jesus came and said to them, 'All authority in heaven and on earth has been given to me. Go therefore and make disciples of all nations, baptizing them in the name of the Father and of the Son and of the Holy Spirit, teaching them to observe all that I have commanded you; and lo, I am with you always, to the close of the age.'

According to Schlatter, Jesus is here set forth as the Living Lord who alone possesses the authority which the Gnostic Redeemers claim to possess: he only has that supernatural force which is born of an immediate vision of the Divine. To Jesus alone has authority been given (not to the Gnostic Redeemers) because he alone has the *gnôsis* which confers this force. Unfortunately the evidence for this theory is non-existent: it is pure conjecture. The resurrection scene in xxviii. 16 ff. is directed, not against Gnostics, but towards Dan. vii. 14, where the ultimate triumph of the Son of Man is pictured. The scene in xxviii. 16 ff. is concerned to assert that Jesus, as Risen Lord, already *is* the victorious Son of Man enthroned on high and now commissioning his envoys to summon the nations to his obedience. He is the fulfilment of the vision of the Son of Man in Dan. vii. 14.

And to him was given dominion and glory and kingdom, that all peoples, nations, and languages should serve him; his dominion is an everlasting dominion, which shall not pass away, and his kingdom one that shall not be destroyed.

The second passage which has often been regarded as directed at Gnosticism is Matt. xi. 27–30.

All things have been delivered to me by my Father; and no one knows the Son except the Father, and no one knows the Father except the Son and any one to whom the Son chooses to reveal him. Come to me, all who labour and are heavy-laden, and I will give you rest. Take my yoke upon you, for I am gentle and lowly in heart, and you will find rest for your souls. For my yoke is easy, and my burden is light.

Here the insistence on the knowledge of God possessed by the Son and the transmission of knowledge by the Son to his own have been taken to be a claim that Jesus is the Lord of a new mystery, who gives knowledge over against that given by the Gnostics. But on evidence which cannot be presented here, it is best to refer this section also to the tradition of the Son of Man in Daniel or Ecclesiasticus: it is *not* over against the Gnostic Redeemer that Jesus is here set, but against the tradition of the Law. 'Take my *yoke* upon you and learn of Me'; that is, *not* the yoke of the old Law but of the Messiah.

The brief survey given above will have revealed that it is not necessary to think of Matthew as dominated by anti-Gnosticism. This was not the reason for his emphasis on the ethical teaching of Jesus. Matthew wrote within a Church that was rent by false teachers, by lawlessness, by failure of love; so-called 'Gnostic' elements may have been present and Matthew may have been combating the substitution of speculative or ecstatic experience for obedience to the law of love, but we cannot assume that Gnosticism particularly determined Matthew's thought and caused him to construct the *SM*.

## B. *The Dead Sea Sect*

The reference just made to Matt. xi. 25–30 leads to a consideration of the second influence which may have led Matthew to formulate the *SM*. This passage, I have argued elsewhere (see my *Christian Origins and Judaism*, 1962), is illumined for us by the newly discovered manuscripts usually referred to as the Dead Sea Scrolls. These Scrolls came, presumably, from a highly organized Nonconformist Sect which had survived into first-century Judaism, and it is now necessary to ask whether influences from the Sect at Qumran have been at work either positively or negatively in Matthew. Was it under the impact of this legalistic group, with its tradition of a teacher of Righteousness, that Matthew came to picture his Lord as a Teacher of Righteousness and made of the teaching of Jesus a Messianic law? The numbers of the sectarians both at Qumran and elsewhere were large. Local units of the Sect were, apparently, organized in tens, but the Sect as a whole was numbered in thousands. One thing is to be particularly emphasized. After A.D. 68, that is, in the period when Matthew was being written, there was very probably a scattering of the members of the Dead Sea

Sect. On that date their headquarters at Qumran were attacked and devastated by the 10th Roman legion in the war of the Romans against the Jews which led to the Fall of Jerusalem in A.D. 70. What became of the Sectarians we do not certainly know, but it is justifiable to think that many of them joined the Church. In any case, apart from a probable influx of Sectarians into the Church after A.D. 68, contact between the Dead Sea Sect and the earliest Christians can be regarded as almost certain and as having increased after the date mentioned. Historical probability points to this, as do the many parallels that have been drawn between so much in the New Testament and the documents of the Sect. Does Matthew reveal echoes of the Sect in any way? We might expect this, particularly since Philo of Alexandria (c. 20 B.C. to c. A.D. 50) connects the Essenes, who were at least very like our sectarians, with Syria, where also we are tempted to locate Matthew.

We must begin with a book published by Professor Krister Stendahl of Harvard in 1954, entitled *The School of St. Matthew*. There is a special emphasis in Matthew on the fulfilment of prophecy and Matthew refers to the fulfilment of the Old Testament in a peculiar way, and in eleven places he uses a somewhat fixed formula to introduce his quotations from the Old Testament. For example, at i. 20 we read:

...behold, an angel of the Lord appeared to him in a dream, saying, 'Joseph, son of David, do not fear to take Mary your wife, for that which is conceived in her is of the Holy Spirit; she will bear a son, and you shall call his name Jesus, for he will save his people from their sins.'

Then Matthew adds at v. 22:

All this took place to fulfil what the Lord had spoken by the prophet: 'Behold, a virgin shall conceive and bear a son, and his name shall be called Emmanuel.'

Or again in ii. 23 we read:

And he went and dwelt in a city called Nazareth, that what was spoken by the prophets might be fulfilled, 'He shall be called a Nazarene.'

Compare with the above the following quotations: ii. 6, 15, 18, 23; iv. 15–16; viii. 17; xii. 18–21; xiii. 35. The form of these quotations in Matthew has caused them to be called 'Formula Quotations'. Stendahl has examined all these in great detail and, as a result of his studies and of a comparison he made of these Matthaean quotations with the use of Scripture in the Dead Sea Sect, he claims that Matthew emerged from a school of interpreters who employed methods of exegesis similar to those employed at Qumran. At least we can say that the work of Brownlee, Bleddyn Roberts, and Stendahl, in particular, makes it possible that Matthew may have acquired his method of using the OT from the Sect. Stendahl's work justifies us in searching for further traces of sectarian influences behind Matthew.

There are many possibilities which can only be mentioned: the idea of perfection in Matt. v. 48: 'You, therefore, must be perfect, as your heavenly Father is perfect', and in xix. 21: the words to the rich young ruler: 'If you would be perfect, go sell what you possess and give to the poor, and you will have treasure in heaven; and come, follow me'—Both quotations recall the literature of the Sect, which was composed of the 'perfect of way'. So also does the reference to knowledge in Matt. xi. 25–30 as I have indicated elsewhere (*Christian Origins and Judaism*, 1962). But I want to point out especially two groups of material where sectarian influences do probably break through in Matthew.

First, there are five passages in Matthew where the evangelist's own peculiar understanding of the Church appears. These are:

(a) xiii. 24–30: The Parable of the Tares

(b) xiii. 47–50: The Parable of the Net

(c) xvi. 17–19: The declaration of Peter as the Rock at Caesarea Philippi

(d) xviii. 15–20: The discipline to be followed among Christians

(e) xxviii. 16–20: The Final Resurrection Scene

The last passage, xxviii. 16–20, deals with the Resurrection. Naturally Matthew here has a specifically Christian reference which the Dead Sea Scrolls lack, so that we can dismiss xxviii. 16–20 from consideration. The other four passages, however, all of which have profound significance for Matthew's conception of the Church, may be taken to suggest reminiscences of something like the sectarian milieu.

One passage only, that dealing with Church discipline in Matt. xviii. 15–20, will be dealt with here. This reads:

If your brother sins against you, go and tell him his fault, between you and him alone. If he listens to you, you have gained your brother. But if he does not listen, take one or two others along with you, that every word may be confirmed by the evidence of two or three witnesses. If he refuses to listen to them, tell it to the church; and if he refuses to listen even to the church, let him be to you as a Gentile and a tax collector. Truly, I say to you, whatever you bind on earth shall be bound in heaven, and whatever you loose on earth shall be loosed in heaven. Again I say to you, if two of you agree on earth about anything they ask, it will be done for them by my Father in heaven. For where two or three are gathered in my name, there am I in the midst of them.

With this compare a passage from DSD (v. 26 ff.):

One shall not speak to his brother in anger or resentment, or with a stiff neck or a hard heart or a wicked spirit; one shall not hate him in the folly of his heart. In his days he shall reprove him and shall not bring upon him iniquity; and also a man shall not bring against his neighbour a word before the masters without having rebuked him before witnesses.

There are obvious differences between these two passages. Nevertheless, the essentials of the procedure for dealing with an offender are the same in each: personal reproof in both is to be followed by that before witnesses, and, further, if necessary before the community, the Church or the Sect, as a whole. The closeness of the parallel cannot be denied and it is reasonable to find behind xviii. 15 ff. a milieu similar to that represented in the Dead Sea Scrolls, a view which is reinforced by the examination of the other ecclesiastical passages to which I have referred.

But one warning must be issued here. In xviii. 19 f. the presence of Jesus among his own is expressed as follows: 'For where two or three are gathered together in my name, there am I in the midst of them.' This recalls a saying of a rabbi, who was possibly a contemporary of Matthew, which reads: 'If two sit together and words of the Law (are spoken) between them, the Divine Presence rests between them' (Mishnah Aboth iii. 2). Thus Matt. xviii. 20 is probably a Christianized bit of Rabbinism. It agrees with this that the style of xviii. 18 is more Rabbinic than Sectarian at this point. It reads: 'Truly I say to you, whatever you bind on earth shall be bound in heaven and whatever you loose on earth shall be loosed in heaven.' The rabbinic parallels to the 'binding and loosing' here referred to are abundant: these are technical Rabbinic terms.

Thus in the passage xviii. 15–20 we find a mixture of Sectarian and strictly Rabbinic terminology. Whether we should infer from it some direct interaction between the sectarians and the Church can be determined only in the light of the confirmatory evidence of other passages. This is of very considerable weight. The possible interaction which is contemplated would arise, presumably, from the presence in the Church of elements influenced by the sectarians or even nurtured by them. Their impact is probably particularly to be noted in the growth of the organization of the Church. One of the problems of Christian history is to explain how the Spirit-filled community of the earliest days of the Church developed into the highly organized Catholic Church of the second and subsequent centuries. At least the possibility is to be entertained that the transition from the organizational simplicity of the primitive Church to Catholicism was expedited, if not to a considerable extent caused, by the incursion into the Church of impulses from the Dead Sea Sectarians. Were I greatly daring I might even suggest that the sectarians captured the Early Church, and thus eventually helped to wrench the Church away from its earliest intention. But this would be to go too far. What concerns us now is that in the ecclesiasticism of Matthew, which is often referred to as incipient Catholicism, influences from the Qumran sectarians are traceable.

But this brings me to the second group of materials where these influences are felt, namely in the *SM*. The hand that shaped the ecclesiasticism of Matthew also shaped the Sermon. Influenced by the Sectarians, the *SM* also offers polemic against them. This will here be illustrated only from two passages:

Matt. v. 21–6:

You have heard that it was said to the men of old, 'You shall not kill; and whoever kills shall be liable to judgment.' But I say to you that every one who is angry with his brother shall be liable to judgment; whoever insults his brother shall be liable to the council, and whoever says, 'You fool!' shall be liable to the hell of fire. So if you are offering your gift at the altar, and there remember that your brother has something against you, leave your gift there before the altar and go; first be reconciled to your brother, and then come and offer your gift. Make friends quickly with your accuser, while you are going with him to court, lest your accuser hand you over to the judge, and the judge to the guard, and you be put in prison; truly, I say to you, you will never get out till you have paid the last penny.

The above passage is composite and there are no clear parallels in the Rabbinic sources to the usages to which it refers. Thus Mishnah Sanhedrin does not note any punishment for anger or for speech that is unseemly. But at this point the Dead Sea Sect becomes pertinent. The following passage from DSD is illuminating [vi. 24–27]:

Now these are the laws by which they shall judge in the communal investigation according to the (following) provisions:...he who answers his fellow with stiff neck or speaks with a quick temper so as to reject the instructions of his comrade by disobeying his fellow who is enrolled before him, (has) taken the law into his own hands, so he shall be fined for one year and be excluded.

Here we do have regulations set forth concerning words uttered in wrath and vilification between members of a religious community, and the punishments deemed appropriate for such. The terms the use of which is condemned are not specifically mentioned, so that we do not here find the exact words, *racha* and *more*. But there are noteworthy parallels to these in DSD at vii. 3, 4, 5, 9, 14. Thus, the words v. 22 *b–c*:

And whosoever shall say to his brother, Raca, shall be in danger of the council,
And whosoever shall say, Thou fool, shall be in danger of hell fire.

—these would come very naturally to a person brought up or influenced by the Qumran sectarians. Possibly Matthew has added them to the words of Jesus. On the other hand, Jesus himself may well have uttered them. He may have had the Pharisees and the sectarians in view. The gradations of speech would point to the Sect; the reference to the Council (sunedrion) points probably to the Synagogue.

Here again we note sectarian and Rabbinic motifs combined.

As to the polemic element in the Sermon, we note v. 43:

You have heard that it was said, 'You shall love your neighbour and hate your enemy.' But I say to you, Love your enemies and pray for those who persecute you...

This verse has always created a problem, because no verses in the OT or in the other Jewish literature were known in which there is a commandment to hate the enemy. But this was inculcated, we now know, in the Dead Sea Sect, and it is possible that Jesus had the sectarians in mind when he uttered these words. He was opposing such words as those which we find in DSD at the very beginning: i. 1 ff.

The *SM*, therefore, shows traces of the impact of the sectarians on the early Christian movement, and the same impact, as we saw, helps us to understand the emergence of ecclesiasticism in Matthew. But the sectarian influence on Matthew must not be overemphasized. Impulses to organization such as we find in the Dead Sea Scrolls appeared elsewhere in Judaism, and, therefore, cannot be exclusively traced to the sectarians. In particular, we must repeat that Rabbinic elements break through in Matthew along with sectarian ones. It would therefore be unwise to look mainly to the direction of the Sect for the key to Matthew's sermon. Matthew is not merely a Manual of Discipline, nor the Sermon merely a catechism, nor the Jesus of the Mount merely a Teacher of Righteousness.

## C. *Jamnia*

In much of the above we have seen that sectarian elements co-exist in Matthew with rabbinic. We now, finally, therefore ask whether what we know as Rabbinic Judaism influenced Matthew by attraction or opposition.

Let us recall the events that led to the emergence of what is called Rabbinic Judaism. During the first century, all through the lifetime of Jesus and Paul, the Jews in Palestine were suffering hardship under Roman rule, and eager to throw off the yoke of the Roman Empire. Led by hot-headed Zealots, they finally broke out in revolt. After a bloody war, lasting from A.D. 66 to 70, the Romans inevitably proved victorious. In A.D. 70 they captured the city of Jerusalem and razed it to the ground. Between the slaughter during the war and the degradation of slavery that followed the war, the end of Judaism and of the Jewish nation seemed to have come. What was it that preserved Judaism, so that it is still a living force in our day? It was chiefly the work of a man named R. Johannan b. Zakkai, who, just before Jerusalem fell, was given permission to found a school in a little out-of-the-way place called Jamnia. Even before the war was over, he had tried to gather around him those Jewish teachers whom he could, so that the tradition of Judaism might be carried on, and by a clever ruse, as the story has it, he succeeded in outwitting Rome and, by founding what looked like a harmless school at Jamnia, saving Judaism. After the fall of Jerusalem the chief rabbis of Judaism gathered at Jamnia and continued their work of studying the Law. Note that this was after A.D. 70, that is, during the period when Matthew was being written. What essentially was the achievement of the rabbis at Jamnia? Let us look at them closely.

Two dangers confronted them, namely, divisions among the Jews themselves and pressures against Judaism from outside, from paganism, Gnosticism and Christianity. The rabbis at Jamnia had first of all to close their own ranks and exclude disruptive influences within Judaism itself. They settled a long standing difference between two rival schools, the House of Hillel and the House of Shammai. A common calendar was established for all Jews, so that the festivals could be uniformly observed; a common liturgy was attempted for the Synagogue; the canon of the OT came to be fixed; the rabbinate was given greater significance and, more important still, beginnings were made in fixing the tradition of Jewish law; the Mishnah, the Jewish code of law, began to take shape. Thus after A.D. 70, after what seemed a total collapse, through the work of the rabbis at Jamnia, Rabbinic Judaism rose imposingly from the ashes of the revolt, an impressively unified force.

At the same time Judaism had to defend itself against enemies from without. In particular, it had to face the growing power of Christianity. For self-defence, the rabbis at Jamnia took certain measures. The formation of the Jewish canon itself was partly a reaction against Christianity; rules of fasting were drawn up for Jews in order to avoid confusion with Christian fasts; a prayer (the Birkath ha-Minim) was inserted in the Synagogue liturgy to make it impossible for Jewish Christians to join in the worship of Judaism. In this and in other ways Judaism marked itself off from Christianity and built a fence around itself.

We now suggest that Matthew was conscious of Jamnia as was Jamnia of the new faith, and that the shadow of Jamnia lies over his Gospel. The evidence for this is of two kinds, general and specific.

(a) Generally then, in the first place, Matthew deliberately sets the Gospel over against Judaism. We saw that, according to some, the structure of Matthew is possibly pentateuchal, its five sections corresponding to the five books of Moses. Even if this view cannot be embraced, that Matthew was concerned to set forth a Christian law over against that of Judaism is clear. Statements made by Jews against Christians are counteracted, for example in the following passages:

Matt. xxvii. 62 ff.:

Next day, that is, after the day of Preparation, the chief priests and the Pharisees gathered before Pilate and said, 'Sir, we remember how that imposter said, while he was still alive, "After three days I will rise again."' Therefore order the sepulchre to be made secure until the third day, lest his disciples go and steal him away, and tell the people, 'He has risen from the dead,' and the last fraud will be worse than the first.' Pilate said to them, 'You have a guard of soldiers; go, make it as secure as you can.' So they went and made the sepulchre secure by sealing the stone and setting a guard.

xxviii. 15:

So they took the money and did as they were directed; and this story has been spread among the Jews to this day.

Christians are very markedly set over against the Jewish community. Thus, for example, in the Beatitudes we are probably to emphasize the pronoun, which has an antithetical effect.

Blessed are the poor in spirit; for *theirs* is the Kingdom of Heaven. Blessed are they that mourn; for *they* shall be comforted, etc.

It is *these* people, we are perhaps to understand, rather than *those*, that is, the Pharisees and Jews who are blessed. In v. 10 the two groups emerge clearly as Christians and Jews:

Blessed are you when men revile you and persecute you and utter all kinds of evil against you falsely on my account.

Then, immediately after the Beatitudes, the verses in v. 13–16 throw the Christian community into a sharp light. This is the salt and light of the world. In v. 13, 14 the *you* again is emphatic. '*You* are the salt of the earth; *you* are the light of the world.' Thus the antithetic motif in the *SM* is *not* confined to the antitheses in v. 21–48. In these, in any case, the ethical demands of Jesus are certainly set over against those of Judaism: '*You have heard that it was said...but I say unto you.*' Six times is this antithesis made clear. And the same motif appears in the rest of the Sermon. In vi. 1–4 Christian practice is contrasted to that which, sometimes at least, goes on in the Synagogue, as for example in vi. 2 on almsgiving.

Thus, when you give alms, sound no trumpet before you, as the hypocrites do in the synagogues and in the streets, that they may be praised by men. Truly, I say to you, they have their reward.

Again, in vi. 5 Christian *prayer* is contrasted with *synagogal* prayer: the '*you*' of vi. 9 is again emphatic:

And in praying do not heap up empty phrases as the Gentiles do; for they think that they will be heard for their many words. Do not be like them, for your Father knows what you need before you ask him. Pray then like this: [literally: Thus then do *you* pray:]

And here the Lord's Prayer may be offered as a direct contrast to the main prayer of the Synagogue, on which it may be modelled. Finally, in vii. 29 the *SM* as a whole is contrasted with the scribal tradition of teaching:

...for he taught them as one who had authority, and not as their scribes.

And in xi. 27–30 Jesus and his yoke are set over against the yoke of the Jewish Law.

Take my yoke upon you, and learn from me; for I am gentle and lowly in heart, and you will find rest for your souls. For my yoke is easy, and my burden is light.

In contrast, that is, to the yoke of Judaism.

So far, however, we have only reiterated what can hardly ever have been seriously questioned, namely, that Matthew emerged in a milieu in which Christianity and Judaism were in sharp opposition. Can we now point to more specific elements which could be taken to indicate the direct pressure of Jamnia, as such, on Matthew? I suggest the following:

(a) In Matt. xii. 77 f. we read:

I tell you, something greater than the temple is here. And if you had known what this means, 'I desire mercy, and not sacrifice,' you would not have condemned the guiltless. For the Son of man is lord of the sabbath.

This quotation, from Hos. vi. 6, is repeated again in Matt. ix. 13. This verse begins with a fixed rabbinic formula, 'Go and learn': 'But go ye and learn what that meaneth, I will have mercy and not sacrifice.' Both verses are added by Matthew in view of a particular situation. It was the fall of the Temple in A.D. 70. The verses strongly recall the teaching of Johannan ben Zakkai, the leader of the Jewish migration to Jamnia.

It is narrated that R. Johannan b. Zakkai was one day going out of Jerusalem accompanied by his disciple R. Joshua b. Hananiah. At the sight of the Temple in ruins Joshua exclaimed, 'Woe to us for the place where the iniquities of Israel were atoned for is destroyed.' Johannan replied: 'Do not grieve my son for we have an atonement which is just as good, namely, deeds of mercy, as the Scripture says, "For I desire mercy and not sacrifice."' ((Hos. vi. 6) Aboth de R. Nathan iv. 5.)

(b) Next there is the structure of the SM itself. It follows a pattern familiar to the rabbis at Jamnia. A famous verse of the rabbis reads as follows:

Simeon the Just was of the remnants of the Great Synagogue. He used to say: By three things is the world sustained: by the Law, by the Temple Service or worship, and by deeds of loving-kindness.

This saying must have echoed often in the walls at Jamnia. They seem to constitute the principles followed by Matthew in his arrangement of the moral foundations of the Christian life. After a declaration of God's grace in the Beatitudes, that is, grace as the foundation of all moral demands in the Gospel, Matthew sets forth the content of the Christian law, so to speak, in v. 17–48: this is the first foundation—Law. He next deals in vi. 1–18 with the nature of true worship: alms, prayer, fasting—this is the second foundation. There then follows miscellaneous material, which has always been difficult to classify, but which can well be comprised under the title: '*deeds of loving-kindness*', the third foundation mentioned by Simeon the Just. Thus the structure of the *SM* is rabbinic.

(*c*) Very significant, further, are minor details which occur in Matthew. At iv. 23, ix. 35, x. 17, xii. 9, xiii. 54, Matthew speaks of 'their synagogues'. This may imply that already the prayer called the *Birkath ha-Minim*, making it very difficult for Christians to share in synagogal worship, has become effective and Christians, for Matthew, are being pushed outside the Synagogue. The title, 'Rabbi', which became more and more important at Jamnia, is deliberately rejected in xxiii. 8: 'But be ye not called Rabbi: for one is your master.' Again in xxiii attention is particularly given to the Pharisees as such, and they were victors at Jamnia.

None of the factors I have listed—the reference to the supremacy of mercy over sacrifice, to the structure of the Sermon, to the sixfold antitheses, and to other minor details—none of these unmistakably refer to Jamnia, but they all, I think, imply an awareness of the Judaism arising there. One difficulty, however, has to be met. Away in a remote little township, such as was Jamnia, did not the rabbinic scholars there go on their way of consolidation and expulsion unnoticed by the Church? And were they, too, in turn indifferent to the Church? I have gone into this question elsewhere in detail. I can here only suggest what seems to me to have been the case, namely, that Jamnia and the Church frequently crossed each other's paths and possibly were in bitter dialogue. The decrees proceeding from Jamnia to all Jewry, the journeyings of its scholars, made Jamnia well known. Much as the World Council of Churches is in the twentieth-century air, so was Jamnia in the air of the late first-century Jewish and Christian life.

And, in part at least, Matthew is the Christian answer to the Judaism emerging at Jamnia. The *SM* is the deliberate formulation of the Christian moral ideal and tradition at a time when the Mishnah was coming to birth in Judaism. The needs of the Church to combat moral laxity in Gnostic or other forms, the incursion into the Church of sectarians from the Dead Sea Sect with their rigid legal emphasis and exegetical and disciplinary tradition, all these factors may have helped to make Matthew emphasize the moral teaching of Jesus. Yet none of these factors singly or together, it seems to me, supply an adequate reason for the truly majestic deliberateness with which Matthew prepared his great manifesto. The *SM* is seen in true perspective only against the Judaism of Jamnia: other factors enter the picture but Jamnia is the chief formative influence. In thus setting the *SM* over against Jamnia, I have to make a leap in imagination which the very strictest adherence to the evidence does not perhaps justify. I can only plead that it seems to me that the facts demand some such leap. Matthew confronted many currents within and without the Church which, as we have seen, influenced him. Nevertheless, what chiefly led him to concentrate on using the words of Jesus himself, sectarian conventions, and rabbinic forms in the *SM* was the desire and necessity to present the ethic of the New Israel, the Church, at a time when the rabbis were engaged in the same task for the Old Israel at Jamnia. In the next chapter we shall ask what forces from within the Church may have influenced Matthew.

*Introduced as 'Background for scripture class.'*

4

# THE SETTING IN THE
# EARLY CHURCH

In the first chapter it was argued that the *SM* presents
Jesus of Nazareth as a second Moses, a giver of a new law
from a new Sinai, and in the second chapter that there
were certain forces at work in the first century, at the
time when Matthew was written, which led to the presentation of Jesus in this light. The peril of immorality,
possibly though not probably of a Gnostic kind, the pressure of Sectarians from a legalistic background and, above
all, the necessity to confront Rabbinic Judaism with a
Christian counterpart, all these factors may have helped
to formulate Matthew's understanding of Jesus and the
Sermon. The question we must now ask is a simple one.
Is the concept of Jesus as a new and greater Moses an
innovation, for which Matthew is himself responsible,
and which indicates a difference between him and the
early Church? Was Matthew alone in his emphasis on
Jesus as lawgiver or were there forces at work inside the
Church which prepared the way for Matthew's interpretation? Did Matthew impress his own Jewish legalism
in a Christian form upon Jesus or was he merely making
more explicit than did others what the Church generally
accepted, namely that Jesus was the New Moses? In
short, what was the setting of the *SM* in the early
Church?

*on Reward*

## A. *Anti-Paulinism*

In the first place, we have to deal with the view that Matthew composed the *SM* in order to combat the influence of Paul on the Church. The Apostle Paul had so strongly emphasized the doctrine of grace, that is, salvation as a free gift of God rather than as a reward for good works, that many Christians, who misunderstood him, had come to think that morality was no part of the Christian life, faith in God's grace alone being necessary. Paulinism, strange to say, had become a menace to morality. This it was that led Matthew, we are told, to emphasize the need for good works in the *SM*.

What is the evidence that Matthew was concerned to refute Paulinism? It rests on the interpretation of a few well-known passages:

(*a*) Matt. v. 18 ff.:

For verily I say unto you, till heaven and earth pass away, one jot or one tittle shall in no wise pass from the law till all will be fulfilled. Whosoever therefore shall break one of these *least* commandments and shall teach men to, he shall be called *the least* in the kingdom of heaven: but whosoever shall do and teach them, the same shall be called great in the kingdom of heaven.

There is here quite clearly a play on the word 'least', and this recalls how Paul describes himself in 1 Cor. xv. 9. 'For I am *the least* of the Apostles, that am not meet to be called an apostle, because I persecuted the Church of God; But by the grace of God I am what I am' (RSV). Thus the phrase '*the least of the apostles*' or 'the least' had come to gain in the early Church—so it is urged—an anti-Pauline undertone. It may even have become a cryptic, sarcastic, designation of Paul himself, a nickname for the Apostle whose Latin name, *Paulus*, meant 'small'. And Matt. v. 19 is intended to attack Paul, who is to be called 'the least' because he has not taught the commandments. Nevertheless, the anti-Paulinism of v. 19 is not to be taken as obvious. The context of v. 19 is not anti-Pauline, and 1 Cor. xv. 9 may have been far removed from Matthew. That Paul's significance may have been known to Matthew we must assume, but that he knew Paul's epistles and 1 Cor. xv. 9 in particular is unlikely. The term 'the least' *may* have been directed against Paul, but the passage cannot certainly be so taken. Unless there is evidence elsewhere in Matthew for anti-Paulinism it would be unwise to detect it in v. 17–19. Is there such evidence?

(2) Appeal is often made to the parable of the *Wheat and the Tares* in xiii. 24–30:

Another parable he put before them, saying, 'The Kingdom of heaven may be compared to a man who sowed good seed in his field; but while men were sleeping, his enemy came and sowed weeds among the wheat, and went away. So when the plants came up and bore grain, then the weeds appeared also. And the servants of the householder came and said to him, "Sir, did you not sow good seed in your field? How then has it weeds?" He said to them, "An enemy has done this." The servants said to him, "Then do you want us to go and gather them?" But he said, "No; lest in gathering the weeds you root up the wheat along with them. Let both grow together until the harvest; and at harvest time I will tell the reapers, Gather the weeds first and bind them in bundles to be burned, but gather the wheat into my barn."'

Here the term 'the enemy man' in xiii. 28 or 'the enemy' in xiii. 25 has been taken to be a cryptic reference to Paul who sowed the seeds of moral indifference in the Church. But in the explanation of the parable that Matthew himself gives, 'the enemy' is identified explicitly in xiii. 36–43 as the Devil. There is therefore no justification for regarding the Matthaean parable as anti-Pauline in its intention.

(3) The next text to be mentioned is Matt. xvi. 17 f.

And Jesus answered him, 'Blessed are you, Simon Bar-Jona! For flesh and blood has not revealed this to you, but my Father who is in heaven. And I tell you, you are Peter, and on this rock I will build my church, and the powers of death shall not prevail against it. I will give you the keys of the kingdom of heaven, and whatever you bind on earth shall be bound in heaven, and whatever you loose on earth shall be loosed in heaven.'

The blessing of Peter here, it has been claimed, is designed to counteract and to depress the claims of Paul as the leader of the Church. But this view again is not necessary. Peter is given the same pre-eminence elsewhere in the NT. The primacy given to Peter among the earliest disciples is not an anti-Pauline peculiarity of Matthew, but typical of the whole tradition.

There is, therefore, no justification for thinking that Matthew has formulated the *SM* in order to oppose the influence of Paul. And, perhaps, the reader has been prompted to ask why any time should have been spent in disputing this point. The answer is twofold. First, to regard the *SM* as a counterblast against Paul is to make it easy to regard it as merely an emphasis on the part of Matthew, a corrective or a polemic which reveals an insight into the meaning of the Gospel less profound than that possessed by his opponents. The anti-Pauline interpretation of the *SM* reduces Matthew to a 'mere moralist'. But secondly, and more important, if Matthew is in opposition to Paul, he stands opposed to one of the most creative and influential figures in the early Church and, moreover, to the earliest figure that we really know in the life of the Church, because the Pauline epistles are earlier than any other NT documents. With Paul we are at the beginnings of the Christian movement, so that if Matthew is far removed from Paul he is very likely to be outside some of the main forces at work in the earliest days of the Church.

We must now, therefore, ask whether, in fact, Paul and

Matthew are far removed in their understanding of the Christian life and of the role of the words of Jesus in that life. Of all the figures of the NT, as we have already suggested, Paul perhaps is the best known, but he is none the less difficult to understand. And, in particular, it is hard to grasp how Paul understood the ethical or moral life of Christians in its relation to his theology. Paul divided his own life clearly into two parts. There was first his life under the Law when he was a Jew; and then, secondly, his life 'in Christ'; the two parts were distinctly separated by his experience on the road to Damascus. The contrast between the two parts at first seems to be a contrast between a life under law and a life under grace, free from Law. The act by which a Christian acknowledged his faith and really began to live 'in Christ' was baptism. This act symbolized for Paul a death to the old life under the Law—a death once and for all—and a rising to a newness of life 'in Christ' or 'in the Spirit'. By baptism the Christian, through faith, had died, had risen, had been justified: he was a new creation. Was there room in his life for anything more and did he now need any law, or could he simply live in spontaneous response to the Spirit under no legal constraint of any kind?

And it has often been stated that there is no room for 'law' in the Christian life as Paul understood it. It was for him a life of freedom in the Spirit. But three factors complicated this 'new life' in Christ, as Paul soon came to recognize. First, although he was a new creation, the Christian man was still in the flesh and therefore still open to the attacks of sin. Secondly, because he was still in the flesh he was also still subject to the hostile supernatural forces which were arraigned against men—the prince of the power of the air, the elements of this world; these were still active and had to be met. And, thirdly, despite his castigation of the works of the Law, Paul never gave up the belief that at the end, in the final consummation, each man would be judged according to his works.

Rom. xiv. 10–12:

Why do you pass judgment on your brother? Or you, why do you despise your brother? For we shall all stand before the judgment seat of God; for it is written, 'As I live, says the Lord, every knee shall bow to me, and every tongue shall give praise to God.' So each of us shall give account of himself to God.

Saved and justified as he was, the Christian was still living between the time of the first appearance of Christ and the End. And so, inevitably, Paul was faced with the question of Christian behaviour. How was a Christian to conduct himself 'betwixt the times' in this world?

To answer this question Paul pursued many paths. He appealed to the imitation of himself in so far as he imitated Christ: he pointed Christians, as we have seen, to the life, death and resurrection of Jesus and urged them to re-enact the life of Jesus in their own lives, to live in Christ, to die and to rise with him. He made use, reluctantly, of what was a well known popular Hellenistic concept, that of 'conscience', to help Christians at Corinth. He also drew upon codes of behaviour which were known in the Hellenistic world and among the Rabbis. Consider the following code used in Col. iii. 16–22:

Let the word of Christ dwell in you richly, as you teach and admonish one another in all wisdom, and as you sing psalms and hymns and spiritual songs with thankfulness in your hearts to God. And whatever you do, in word or deed, do everything in the name of the Lord Jesus, giving thanks to God the Father through him.

*Wives, be subject to your* husbands, as is fitting in the Lord. *Husbands,* love your wives, and do not be harsh with them. *Children,* obey your parents in everything, for this pleases the Lord. *Fathers,* do not provoke your children, lest they become discouraged. *Slaves*, obey in everything those who are your earthly masters, not with eyeservice, as men-pleasers, but in singleness of heart, fearing the Lord.

With these matters, however, we cannot now stay, because what is especially important for us is that he also appealed to the very words of Jesus for moral guidance. This appears in two ways: a careful reading of the Pauline Epistles reveals again and again that there are echoes of the Sayings of Jesus constantly creeping into the apostle's words. For example it has been estimated that at over a thousand points the words of Paul recall those of Jesus. Let me quote one example from the Epistle to the Romans, compare:

| Rom. xii. 14 | Matt. v. 44 |
|---|---|
| Bless those who persecute you; bless and do not curse them. | But I say to you, Love your enemies and pray for those who persecute you. |

| Rom. xii. 17 | Matt. v. 39 ff. |
|---|---|
| Repay no one evil for evil, but take thought for what is noble in the sight of all. | But I say to you, Do not resist one who is evil. But if any one strikes you on the right cheek, turn to him the other also; and if any one would sue you and take your coat, let him have your cloak as well; and if any one forces you to go one mile, go with him two miles. Give to him who begs from you, and do not refuse him who would borrow from you. |

| Rom. xiii. 7 | Mark xii. 13–17 |
|---|---|
| Pay all of them their dues, taxes to whom taxes are due, revenue to whom revenue is due, respect to whom respect | And they sent to him some of the Pharisees and some of the Herodians, to entrap him in his talk. And they came and |

Rom. xiii. 7 (*cont.*)

is due, honour to whom honour is due.

Mark xii. 13–17 (*cont.*)

said to him, 'Teacher, we know that you are true, and care for no man; for you do not regard the position of men, but truly teach the way of God. Is it lawful to pay taxes to Caesar, or not? Should we pay them, or should we not?' But knowing their hypocrisy, he said to them, 'Why put me to the test? Bring me a coin, and let me look at it.' And they brought one. And he said to them, 'Whose likeness and inscription is this?' They said to him, 'Caesar's.' Jesus said to them, 'Render to Caesar the things that are Caesar's, and to God the things that are God's.' And they were amazed at him.

Rom. xiii. 8–10

Owe no one anything, except to love one another; for he who loves his neighbour has fulfilled the law. The commandments, 'You shall not commit adultery, You shall not kill, You shall not steal, You shall not covet,' and any other commandment, are summed up in this sentence, 'You shall love your neighbour as yourself.' Love does no wrong to a neighbour; therefore love is the fulfilling of the law.

Mark xii. 28–34

And one of the scribes came up and heard them disputing with one another, and seeing that he answered them well, asked him, 'Which commandment is the first of all?' Jesus answered, 'The first is, "Hear, O Israel: The Lord our God, the Lord is one; and you shall love the Lord your God with all your heart, and with all your soul, and with all your mind, and with all your strength." The second is this, "You shall love your neighbour as yourself." There is no other

Mark xii. 28–34 (*cont.*)

commandment greater than
these.' And the scribe said to
him, 'You are right, Teacher;
you have truly said that he is
one, and there is no other
but he; and to love him with
all the heart, and with all
the understanding, and with
all the strength, and to love
one's neighbour as oneself, is
much more than all whole
burnt offerings and sacrifices.'
And when Jesus saw that he
answered wisely, he said to
him, 'You are not far from
the kingdom of God.' And
after that no one dared to ask
him any question.

Rom. xiv. 10

Why do you pass judgment on
your brother? Or you, why
do you despise your brother?
For we shall all stand before
the judgment seat of God.

(and)

Rom. xiv. 13

Then let us no more pass judgment on one another, but
rather decide never to put a
stumbling block or hindrance
in the way of a brother.

Matt. vii. 1

'Judge not, that you be not
judged.'

This means that Paul was steeped in the tradition of what
Jesus had said and that the words of Jesus had become
bone of his bone. It is erroneous to think that Paul was
not interested in the details of the life of Jesus: his moral
awareness, at least, was rooted in the teaching of Jesus
about the good life.

But even more significant than the unconscious echoes of Jesus' words in the Epistles is the way in which Paul actually quotes the words of Jesus and treats them as finally authoritative. This appears clearly from 1 Corinthians where the apostle distinguishes between his own opinions and the words of Jesus Himself.

1 Cor. vii. 10:

To the married I give charge, not I but the Lord, that the wife should not separate from her husband (but if she does, let her remain single or else be reconciled to her husband)—and that the husband should not divorce his wife.

1 Cor. ix. 14:

In the same way, the Lord commanded that those who proclaim the gospel should get their living by the gospel.

1 Cor. xiv. 37:

If any one thinks that he is a prophet, or spiritual, he should acknowledge that what I am writing to you is a command of the Lord.

Paul like Matthew, then, knows and appeals to the words of Jesus. And this is precisely what we ought to expect. Because, as for Matthew, so for Paul, there was a real correspondence between the Christian dispensation and the events of the Exodus. The redemption of Israel from Egypt was the prototype of the greater redemption from sin wrought by Christ. Thus Christ for Paul also had the lineaments of a new and greater Moses and His words were regarded by him as binding upon Christians. It is not necessary to labour the obvious. Paul and Matthew share a common understanding over a large area of Christ and his words. Thus the *SM* would not strike Paul as an alien importation into the faith; like Matthew Paul too can speak of a law of Christ, which is partly at least composed of Jesus' words: he is 'in the law of Christ'.

## Gal. vi. 2:

Bear one another's burdens, and so fulfil the law of Christ.

## 1 Cor. ix. 9–23:

For it is written in the law of Moses, 'You shall not muzzle an ox when it is treading out the grain.' Is it for oxen that God is concerned? Does he not speak entirely for our sake? It was written for our sake, because the plowman should plow in hope and the thresher thresh in hope of a share in the crop. If we have sown spiritual good among you, is it too much if we reap your material benefits? If others share this rightful claim upon you, do not we still more?

Nevertheless, we have not made use of this right, but we endure anything rather than put an obstacle in the way of the gospel of Christ. Do you not know that those who are employed in the temple service get their food from the temple, and those who serve at the altar share in the sacrificial offerings? In the same way, the Lord commanded that those who proclaim the gospel should get their living by the gospel.

But I have made no use of any of these rights, nor am I writing this to secure any such provision. For I would rather die than have any one deprive me of my ground for boasting. For if I preach the gospel, that gives me no ground for boasting. For necessity is laid upon me. Woe to me if I do not preach the gospel! For if I do this of my own will, I have a reward; but if not of my own will, I am entrusted with a commission. What then is my reward? Just this: that in my preaching I may make the gospel free of charge, not making full use of my right in the gospel.

*For though I am free from all men, I have made myself a slave to all, that I might win the more. To the Jews I became as a Jew, in order to win Jews; to those under the law I became as one under the law—though not being myself under the law—that I might win those under the law. To those outside the law I became as one outside the law—not being without law toward God but under the law of Christ—that I might win those outside the law. To the weak I became weak, that I might win the weak. I have become all things to all men, that I might by all means save some. I do it all for the sake of the gospel, that I may share in its blessings.* [Our italics.]

## B. *Q: radicalism*

But, turning away from Paul, can we trace the same reverence for the words of Jesus elsewhere before Matthew's time? Let us look now upon the two sources upon which the *SM* has drawn. And the first source to be examined is that entitled Q, which, in written or oral form, goes back probably to about A.D. 50. The symbol Q stands for the material in the tradition which was common to Matthew and Luke: we isolate it here for convenience, and only its main emphases will be noted.

Several reasons have been given for the preservation and transmission of the words of Jesus in Q. Christians, it has been rightly claimed, would naturally be eager to recall what Jesus had done and said merely because He had become for them the Lord. They would also want to use the same words for hortatory purposes in the Church, at baptism and in sermons; moreover, in its confrontation with Judaism, the Church would have found the impressive moral teaching of Jesus a powerful weapon, as it was also for apologetic purposes in dealing with those sections of the Gentile world which were casting about for a moral and spiritual basis for society. Most scholars, both form critics and others, have emphasized the hortatory and catechetical impulses as leading to the preservation of Q. In this T. W. Manson, Vincent Taylor and Dibelius are all agreed. Exhortation and catechism were the main channels for the preservation of the tradition which we find in Q. Accordingly it is best to think of Q as a kind of Christian book of Proverbs inculcating the good life. And in the light of historical probability and of the express witness of Paul, who as we saw treated the words of Jesus as hortatory material, it would be idle to deny the catechetical and exhortatory value of Q. Exhortation breaks through expressly in Q material at Luke xi. 35, xii. 40. Thus xi. 35 reads: 'Therefore be careful lest the light in you be darkness.' And in xii. 40 (Matt. xiv. 35) we read: 'You also must be ready; for the Son of man is coming at an hour you do not expect.'

Are we then to conclude that the early Church first preserved the teaching of Jesus because it discovered its catechetical value, or, to put it in other words, because it was useful for the moral instruction of converts? Before we draw this conclusion certain facts must be borne in mind.

(*a*) Form critics have isolated in the Gospel tradition certain stories and units of tradition which were useful for purposes of preaching in the early Church in that they supplied answers to difficulties confronting the early Church. These stories or units of tradition have been called by different names by different scholars. (Bultmann calls them *apophthegmata*: Dibelius, *paradeigmata*.) Vincent Taylor's term for them explains itself: he called them Pronouncement stories because they reached their climax in a solemn utterance or pronouncement by Jesus. Let us take one example of such a story:

One sabbath he was going through the grainfields; and as they made their way his disciples began to pluck ears of grain. And the Pharisees said to him, 'Look, why are they doing what is not lawful on the sabbath?' And he said to them, 'Have you never read what David did, when he was in need and was hungry, he and those who were with him: how he entered the house of God, when Abiathar was high priest, and ate the bread of the Presence, which it is not lawful for any but the priests to eat, and also gave it to those who were with him?' And he said to them, 'The sabbath was made for man, not man for the sabbath; so the Son of man is lord even of the sabbath.' (Mark ii. 23–8.)

Now stories such as this, pronouncement stories, were eminently hortatory. It is fair to argue that if Q was intended to be hortatory and catechetical we should expect it to contain a fair sprinkling of such stories. But out of all the pronouncement stories listed by Dibelius, Bultmann and Taylor only about five at the outside appear in Q material. In a source designed to be hortatory we should expect hortatory stories. These we do *not* find in Q.

(*b*) We have referred to exhortatory passages that do occur in Q. But it also needs to be stated that many passages in Q which have been claimed to be hortatory turn out on examination not to be such, or at least their intention is not likely originally to have been catechetical or exhortatory. For example, Dibelius takes Matt. v. 44–8 and vi. 25–31 to be exhortation. They read:

But I say to you, Love your enemies and pray for those who perse-cute you, so that you may be sons of your Father who is in heaven; for he makes his sun rise on the evil and on the good, and sends rain on the just and on the unjust. For if you love those who love you, what reward have you? Do not even the tax collectors do the same? And if you salute only your brethren, what more are you doing than others? Do not even the Gentiles do the same? You, therefore, must be perfect, as your heavenly Father is perfect. (Matt. v. 44–8.)

'Therefore I tell you, do not be anxious about your life, what you shall eat or what you shall drink, nor about your body, what you shall put on. Is not life more than food, and the body more than clothing? Look at the birds of the air: they neither sow nor reap nor gather into barns, and yet your heavenly Father feeds them. Are you not of more value than they? And which of you by being anxious can add one cubit to his span of life? And why are you anxious about clothing? Consider the lilies of the field, how they grow; they neither toil nor spin; yet I tell you, even Solomon in all his glory was not arrayed like one of these. But if God so clothes the grass of the field, which today is alive and tomorrow is thrown into the oven, will he not much more clothe you, O men of little faith? Therefore do not be anxious, saying, 'What shall we eat?' or 'What shall we drink?' or 'What shall we wear?' (Matt. vi. 25–31.)

In a generalized sense it is certainly permissible to classify these two passages as hortatory and catechetical, and doubtless Matthew has so used them, but it will also be agreed that their content is so exalted that their meaning, no less than their form, does not suggest the pedestrian purposes we usually associate with catechetical instruction and exhortation. They are far removed from anything like the prudential maxims of a book of Proverbs.

(*c*) But more pointed still is a third fact. We have stated that Q has been claimed to be catechetical. If this be in truth the case, then we should be able to assume that much of the tradition of the words of Jesus has come down to us along catechetical channels and that the formulary marks of those channels should be discoverable in Q. Fortunately we can put this assumption to the test. Much of the catechetical material which has found its way from the early Church into the New Testament has been recently isolated. We now know that a great deal in the Epistles of Paul, in 1 Peter, in James is derived from a pattern of catechism which was widely employed in various forms in the early Church. The late Dean E. G. Selwyn of Winchester urged that behind many of the New Testament writers there was a catechetical tradition dealing with the following themes (code (*c*) does not here concern us) (see his commentary on 1 Peter, London, 1946):

(*a*) Holiness as befitted the people of God
(*b*) The children of the light
(*c*) The nature of Baptism
(*d*) The new life in Christ, its renunciations
(*e*) The faith and worship of the new life
(*f*) Various virtues
(*g*) Church unity and Church order
(*h*) The subordination of Christians
(*i*) Civil obedience
(*j*) Slaves, masters, wives, husbands, children

There are traces of a persecution catechism. For our particular purposes these deserve quotation. They are: 1 Thess. i. 6; ii. 4, 14; iii. 2–5; v. 1–3, 4–11, 17–19; iii. 8; 2 Thess. i. 4–7, 10; ii. 15; 1 Pet. i. 6–7, 10–11, 13, 21; ii. 4–5, 8–9, 12, 20–1, 24; iii. 14–15; iv. 3, 5, 7, 12–13, 17–19; v. 4, 8–10, 12; Acts i. 7; v. 41; xiv. 22; xx. 28; 1 Cor. i. 7–9; iii. 13; vii. 29; xvi. 13; 2 Cor. viii. 2; Heb. x. 23, 30, 32–3; Jas. i. 2–3, 12; iv. 7; v. 8; Rom. ii. 5–11;

v. 2, 3–4; xiii. 11, 13–14; Phil. i. 27–9; iv. 1; 2 Pet. ii. 10; Rev. xvi. 15; Col. iv. 2–3, 12; Eph. i. 14; vi. 14 ff.

The important fact is this: when the catechetical elements in the New Testament are compared with Q, in only one section are there any serious parallels between them: Q would therefore *not* seem to be catechetical in its main intent. On the other hand an examination of all the material in Q, as far as we can reconstruct it, or as far as it is preserved, reveals that Q brings two things into prominence, the crisis which the coming of Christ constitutes and the significance of his person.

Parallels to the above materials are found according to Selwyn in the following passages from Q (those marked P are only possibly from Q): (1) Matt. v. 10–12 (= Luke vi. 22); (2) Luke xx. 35; (3) Luke vi. 32 f.; (4) Luke xxii. 28; (5) Mark xiii. 13 (P); (6) Matt. xiii. 7 (P); (7) Mark xiii. 11 (P); (8) Matt. x. 28 (= Luke xii. 45); (9) Mark xiii. 32 f. (P); (10) Luke xii. 39–40 (compare Matt. xxiv. 43 f.) (P); (11) Luke xxi. 34 (P); (12) Mark xiii. 8 (= Matt. xxiv. 8) (P); (13) Matt. x. 32 f. (= Luke xii. 8, 9) (P); (14) Luke xxi. 36 (= Matt. vi. 13) (P); (15) Luke xii. 35 (P); (16) Mark xiii. 33, 35–7 (P); (17) Matt. xxv. 13 (P). There are also parallels to Synoptic materials from Matt. x. 25; Luke xvii. 7; Mark xiii. 27; viii. 38.

Apart from the examples we have given, a glance at the material in Q as a whole confirms its crisis character. Thus it begins with the advent of John the Baptist. There is a wrath to come: the axe is laid at the root of the tree. Immediately following the story of the Baptist, Jesus emerges as the Son of God in his own baptism and in his temptation. The opening of Q is, thus, eschatological and Christological. The final process of history has begun: the final repentance is demanded: there is a judgement on the old Israel and a new Israel is being gathered (see Matt. iii .12):

His winnowing fork is in his hand, and he will clear his threshing floor and gather his wheat into the granary, but the chaff he will burn with unquenchable fire.

The next material in Q consists of the Beatitudes. Dibelius takes these to be exhortatory, but they are rather designed to set forth the crisis, which is the coming of Christ, in its aspect of promise. Indeed, on full scrutiny, the sound of the axe of crisis is heard throughout Q: it seems to be concerned not with the normalities of catechetical instruction: it has a crisis character and expresses the total, final demand that God lays upon men. One word to describe the teaching preserved in Q would be *radical*. It presents an absolute ethic concerned to register the immediate impact of the divine demand, uninfluenced by the contingencies of experience or the crippling realities of circumstances. Thus the words of Jesus in Q attest two things: the uncompromising character of their claim, in its nakedness, and, at the same time, the moral enthusiasm of the first Christians, the first fine careless rapture of the early Christian community, which confronted and dared the impossible, as the experiment in voluntary 'communism' in Acts reveals. Doubtless Q preserves the way of life demanded by Jesus while he was on earth and often attempted by the earliest Christians under the initial impact of the life, death and resurrection of Jesus. Q expresses not a catechism but a cataclysmic crisis: not the currents of custom but the Niagara of a new beginning— a metaphor I owe to Professor Amos N. Wilder.

As you will remember, however, the primitive experiment in communism proved short-lived. Soon it became necessary to send money to the poor of Jersusalem who had used their capital unwisely. The harsh reality had to be faced that the crisis inaugurated by Jesus had not issued in a new heaven and a new earth. The advent of the Lord, when he was finally to introduce a new order, was delayed. The enthusiasts of the Day of Pentecost had to go out into a cold world to face again on an old earth the light of common day. Enthusiasm proved not to be enough.

Let us look at the situation as we find it in our earliest sources, again the Pauline Epistles. Christians at Thessalonica, thinking that the Day of the Lord, which would wind up all things, was at hand, had come to think that work was no longer necessary: the Lord was at hand, to labour was superfluous. But, with what has been called his 'robust common sense', Paul issued an injunction to them that those who did not work should neither eat. In short, he calls upon them to recognize the actualities of existence in this world; the ethic of crisis had to be adapted to the humdrum affairs of life. The contemplation of the lilies of the field that toiled not nor spun had to be reconciled with the necessity to maintain life and to labour. The teaching of Q had to be applied. And the process whereby this application of an impossible ethic began is seen most clearly in the other material which we found behind the *SM*, that designated as M, to which we now turn.

## C. *M: regulation*

In two ways the teaching of Jesus in M, although it, too, preserves the crisis character of the words of Jesus in the intensity of their demand, nevertheless shows how these *radical* words begin to take on a *regulatory* character, that is, they become used as guides for the actual business of living.

In the first place, whereas the teaching of Jesus in Q is set out in relation to the ministry of John the Baptist, that is, in a context of crisis, M relates the teaching of Jesus to

Judaism. The words of Jesus are compared with those of the ancient Jewish worthies. This comparison antedates M itself and probably goes back to the very earliest days of the Church, if not to Jesus himself. The point to note here is that the antithetical form of M's presentation of the words of Jesus over against Judaism has in fact the effect of characterizing them as a new law which has fulfilled the old. It is so that Matthew understood the antitheses, as we saw before, and at this point, therefore, he did not innovate. There can be little doubt that the confrontation of the words of Jesus with Judaism in M did provide for the possibility of the legal understanding of the words of Jesus, that is, for their use in a regulatory fashion.

But, in the second place, M itself explicitly treated the words of Jesus in a regulatory manner. Let us consider the following passages:

(a) Matt. v. 27–32:

'You have heard that it was said, "You shall not commit adultery." But I say to you that everyone who looks at a woman lustfully has already committed adultery with her in his heart. If your right eye causes you to sin, pluck it out and throw it away...

'It was also said, 'Whoever divorces his wife, let him give her a certificate of divorce.' But I say to you that everyone who divorces his wife, except on the ground of unchastity [adultery], makes her an adulteress; and whoever marries a divorced woman commits adultery....'

The phrase 'except for adultery' really makes of Jesus' total prohibition of divorce a principle to be applied in a regulatory fashion, that is, it is brought within the realm of the practicable and 'legalized'.

(b) The same interest in the application of Jesus' ethic appears in the passage which follows the discussion of divorce, derived from Mark, in Matt. xix. 1–12. The whole section reads as follows:

Now when Jesus had finished these sayings, he went away from Galilee and entered the region of Judea beyond the Jordan; and large crowds followed him, and he healed them there.

And Pharisees came up to him and tested him by asking, 'Is it lawful to divorce one's wife for any cause?' He answered, 'Have you not read that he who made them from the beginning made them male and female and said, "For this reason a man shall leave his father and mother and be joined to his wife, and the two shall become one"? So they are no longer two but one. What therefore God has joined together, let no man put asunder.' They said to him, 'Why then did Moses command one to give a certificate of divorce, and to put her away?' He said to them, 'For your hardness of heart Moses allowed you to divorce your wives, but from the beginning it was not so. And I say to you: whoever divorces his wife, except for unchastity, and marries another, commits adultery.'

*The disciples said to him, 'If such is the case of a man with his wife, it is not expedient to marry.' But he said to them, 'Not all men can receive this precept, but only those to whom it is given. For there are eunuchs who have been so from birth, and there are eunuchs who have been made eunuchs by men, and there are eunuchs who have made themselves eunuchs for the sake of the kingdom of heaven. He who is able to receive this, let him receive it.'* [Our italics.]

These words italicized in the above form what the Rabbis might have called *Gemara*, an explanatory addition or comment. They do not arise naturally out of xix. 1–9. Rather they reflect the problem of the practicability of the ethic of Jesus as M understands it. In the judgement of M, the ethic of Jesus is not to be applied absolutely and indiscriminately to all alike. In its utterly 'radical' form it can only apply to him 'who is able to stand it' or 'to those to whom it is given to do so'. The generality of men are not to be submitted to it.

(*c*) Similarly in xix. 16–22 Matthew is concerned with the same problem.

And behold, one came up to him, saying, 'Teacher, what good deed must I do, to have eternal life?' And he said to him, 'Why do you ask me about what is good? One there is who is good. If you would enter life, keep the commandments.' He said to him, 'Which?' And Jesus said, 'You shall not kill. You shall not commit adultery, You shall not steal, You shall not bear false witness, Honour your father and mother, and, You shall love your neighbour as yourself.' The young man said to him, 'All these I have observed; what do I still lack?' Jesus said to him, 'If you would be perfect, go, sell what you possess and give to the poor, and you will have treasure in heaven; and come, follow me.' When the young man heard this he went away sorrowful; for he had great possessions.

Here, into a passage derived from Mark, Matthew has introduced the idea that there are grades of achievement in the Christian life. The counsel to sell all and give to the poor is designed only for the perfect: it is not meant to be applied to all. The point of this passage is not to introduce into the Church two orders of morality but to recognize that the commandment of Jesus discriminates; it respects individual differences among men.

(*d*) Again, in Matt. xix. 13–15—

Then children were brought to him that he might lay his hands on them and pray. The disciples rebuked the people; but Jesus said, 'Let the children come to me, and do not hinder them; for to such belongs the kingdom of heaven.' And he laid his hands on them and went away.

—as in its parallel in Mark, we find the same concern to understand what the moral demands of Jesus imply. Did they allow for the bringing up of children? Could one who was to take as his aim the kind of indifference to toil and labour that we find in the lily of the field—could he assume the responsibilities of fatherhood? The disciples are tempted to a negative answer, but their Lord reassures them.

(*e*) Again in an earlier section the concern for actualities emerges in xvii. 22–7.

As they were gathering in Galilee, Jesus said to them, 'The Son of man is to be delivered into the hands of men, and they will kill him, and he will be raised on the third day.' And they were greatly distressed.

*When they came to Capernaum, the collectors of the half-shekel tax went up to Peter and said, 'Does not your teacher pay the tax?' He said, 'Yes.' And when he came home, Jesus spoke to him first, saying, 'What do you think, Simon? From whom do kings of the earth take toll or tribute? From their sons or from others?' And when he said, 'From others,' Jesus said to him, 'Then the sons are free. However, not to give offence to them, go to the sea and cast a hook, and take the first fish that comes up, and when you open its mouth you will find a shekel; take that and give it to them for me and for yourself.'*

This section italicized in the above at first sight is un-related to what precedes. But, on closer examination, it turns out to be an explanatory addition to xvii. 22–3. There the powers of this world are predicted to kill the Son of Man. What then should be the attitude of Chris-tians towards such powers? Should it be one of stark rejection or wise tolerance? In xvii. 24–7 we are given the answer. No offence is to be given to the powers that be.

(*f*) In the following chapter we find instructions given concerning the actual life of the Church: xviii. 15–20 and xviii. 21–35 are relevant.

Matt. xviii. 15–20:

'If your brother sins against you, go and tell him his fault, between you and him alone. If he listens to you, you have gained your brother. But if he does not listen, take one or two others along with you, that every word may be confirmed by the evidence of two or three wit-nesses. If he refuses to listen to them, tell it to the church; and if he refuses to listen even to the church, let him be to you as a Gentile and a tax collector. Truly, I say to you, whatever you bind on earth shall be bound in heaven, and whatever you loose on earth shall be loosed in heaven. Again I say to you, if two of you agree on earth about anything they ask, it will be done for them by my Father in heaven. For where two or three are gathered in my name, there am I in the midst of them.'

Matt. xviii. 21–35:

Then Peter came up and said to him, 'Lord, how often shall my brother sin against me, and I forgive him? As many as seven times?' Jesus said to him, 'I do not say to you seven times, but seventy times seven.'

'Therefore the kingdom of heaven may be compared to a king who wished to settle accounts with his servants. When he began the reckoning, one was brought to him who owed him ten thousand talents; and as he could not pay, his lord ordered him to be sold, with his wife and children and all that he had, and payment to be made. So the servant fell on his knees, imploring him, "Lord, have patience with me, and I will pay you everything." And out of pity for him the lord of that servant released him and forgave him the debt. But that same servant, as he went out, came upon one of his fellow servants who owed him a hundred denarii; and seizing him by the throat, he said, "Pay what you owe." So his fellow servant fell down and besought him, "Have patience with me, and I will pay you." He refused and went and put him in prison till he should pay the debt. When his fellow servants saw what had taken place, they were greatly distressed, and they went and reported to their lord all that had taken place. Then his lord summoned him and said to him, "You wicked servant! I forgave you all that debt because you besought me; and should not you have had mercy on your fellow servant, as I had mercy on you?" And in anger his lord delivered him to the jailers, till he should pay all his debt. So also my heavenly Father will do to every one of you, if you do not forgive your brother from your heart.'

In both sections, xviii. 15 and xviii. 21, 22, we find a bit of Q material followed by several verses from M. These verses again constitute additional explanatory material. Thus xviii. 15 ff. really annuls the too literal understanding of vii. 1, which had forbidden all judging of others (and the same is the function of the verse in vii. 6 forbidding the casting of pearls before swine). Matthew spells out the way in which such an absolute prohibition is to work out in the practical life of the Church. But, lest he should have become too disciplinary, Matthew also adds in xviii. 21–2 the command to forgive seventy times seven, which we have already quoted above.

The above words, in turn, must have caused much heart-searching in the early Church, as it has done to all Christians ever since, and it is therefore followed by a parable from M, in xviii. 23–35, to explain what is meant: the forgiveness demanded must be from the heart.

'So also my heavenly Father will do to every one of you, if you do not forgive your brother from your heart.'

In all the passages referred to above an attempt is made to turn Jesus into a practical legislator who had his feet on the ground: the radicalism of his absolute ethic is being softened. It agrees with this that the Church, as it emerges in Matthew, is a society in which a tradition is handed on which has to be interpreted. Scribes are to be found in it and there is constantly going on a process of 'binding and loosing', of allowing certain things to be done and of forbidding other things. Peter emerges particularly as the Christian counterpart of a Jewish rabbi who has to interpret the words of Christ (xviii. 21). But, as we have seen, this same tendency to rabbinize Christianity is not peculiar to Matthew. It appears even in Paul. Thus in his discussion of marriage Paul virtually tells the Christians at Corinth that, in view of the shortness of the time before the Second Coming of the Lord, it would be wise to avoid marriage. But he goes on to point out, exactly as does Matthew, that not all are capable of this. He introduces a note of practicality into his advice. Consider the following passage:

I Cor. vii. 1–9:

Now concerning the matters about which you wrote. It is well for a man not to touch a woman. But because of the temptation to immorality, each man should have his own wife and each woman her own husband. The husband should give to his wife her conjugal rights, and likewise the wife to her husband. For the wife does not rule over her own body, but the husband does; likewise the husband does not rule over his own body, but the wife does. Do not refuse one another except perhaps by agreement for a season, that you may devote yourselves to prayer; but then come together again, lest Satan tempt you through lack of self-control. I say this by way of concession, not of command. I wish that all were as I myself am. But each has his own special gift from God, one of one kind and one of another.

To the unmarried and widows I say that it is well for them to remain single as I do. But if they cannot exercise self-control, they should marry. For it is better to marry than to be aflame with passion.

Similarly in Rom. xii in a passage which contains many echoes of the absolute standards of the *SM* we read in xii. 18: 'If it be possible, as much as lieth in you, live peaceably with all men.'

"Love"

### D. *The Fourth Gospel: the one principle, Agapê* 7:12

We have surveyed above the two sources upon which the *SM* chiefly draws. While the distinction between them must not be made into a hard and fast one, they do roughly reveal a twofold awareness of an approach to the words of Jesus. In the first block, Q (although it would be unwise to define the material too precisely in terms of specific sources), it is the absolute character of the words of Jesus which is most marked, their *radical* impact. It presents the teaching of Jesus as it came to his disciples, perhaps in its utter nakedness, during his actual ministry, when he called his own to forsake all and to follow him. It would not be misleading to think of Q as reflecting the pre-Easter, and immediately post-Easter, period of the Church. In the second block of material, designated M, there is an attempt made to make applicable these words to the problems of daily living. There is a recognition of what is possible and impossible, absolute and relative. M more than Q, we may claim, reflects, among other things, the experience of the early Church sometime after Easter, when the blinding light of the ministry and Resurrection was past and the Church had emerged as a community in the world which had to take the words of Jesus, not merely as historically interesting, but as valid for its own life. The Church had to consider what this validity meant. In the process it took what was radical, modified it and made it regulatory. The process wherein this happened is contained and continued in the Christian rabbinism of Matthew, where we see slowly emerging a neo-legalistic society.

On the other hand, however, there was also another force at work in the early Church which would subsume the ethical teaching of Jesus under one all-embracing principle. This co-existed with the tendency to make of the words of Jesus a new Law. The use of a summary principle is apparent even in Matthew itself. At the climax of his treatment of the Christian law, Christian worship and Christian lovingkindness, Matthew has placed vii. 12, which is known as the Golden Rule. 'So whatever you wish that men would do to you, do so to them; for this is the law and the prophets.' Similarly the love of God and of the neighbour is made the summation of the Law in Mark xii. 28 with its parallel in Matt. xxii. 35–40, which reads:

| Mark xii. 28 | Matt. xxii. 35–40 |
|---|---|
| And one of the scribes came up and heard them disputing with one another, and seeing that he answered them well, asked him, 'Which commandment is the first of all?' | And one of them, a lawyer, asked him a question, to test him. 'Teacher, which is the great commandment in the law?' And he said to him, 'You shall love the Lord your God with all your heart, and with all your soul, and with all your mind. This is the great and first commandment. And a second is like it, You shall love your neighbor as yourself. On these two commandments depend all the law and the prophets.' |

Paul also knows the law of love as the essence of the demand of God, as in Rom. xiii. 8–10. 'Owe no one anything, except to love one another; for he who loves his neighbour has fulfilled the law. The commandments, "You shall not commit adultery, You shall not kill, You shall not steal, You shall not covet," and any other commandment, are summed up in this sentence, "You shall love your neighbor as yourself." Love does no wrong to a neighbour; therefore love is the fulfilling of the law.' Again, in Gal. v. 14, Paul writes, 'For the whole law is fulfilled in one word, "You shall love your neighbor as yourself"'; and in Col. iii. 14, 'And above all these put on love, which binds everything together in perfect harmony.' The same emerges in Jas. ii. 8, which otherwise appeals to the words of Jesus at least indirectly; here we read: 'If you really fulfil the royal law, according to the scripture, "You shall love your neighbor as yourself," you do well.'

But one striking point is to be noticed in all these extra-Synoptic references. They refer to the love of neighbour, *but not to the love of God.* Only in 1 John iv. 21 is this conjunction made with specific reference to the teaching of Jesus. It reads: 'And this commandment we have from him, that he who loves God should love his brother also.' Why is it that, apart from 1 John iv. 21, the law of love, outside the Gospels of Matthew, Mark and Luke, has no reference to the love of God but only to the love of neighbour? The context of the verse in 1 John iv. 21 supplies the answer:

Beloved, let us love one another; for love is of God, and he who loves is born of God and knows God. He who does not love does not know God; for God is love. In this the love of God was made manifest among us, that God sent his only Son into the world, so that we might live through him. In this is love, not that we loved God but that he loved us and sent His Son to be the expiation for our sins. Beloved, if God so loved us, we also ought to love one another. No man has ever seen God; if we love one another, God abides in us and his love is perfected in us.

By this we know that we abide in him and he in us, because he
has given us of his own Spirit. And we have seen and testify that the
Father has sent his Son as the Savior of the world. Whoever con-
fesses that Jesus is the Son of God, God abides in him, and he in God.
So we know and believe the love God has for us. God is love, and he
who abides in love abides in God, and God abides in him. In this is
love perfected with us, that we may have confidence for the day of
judgment, because as he is so are we in this world. There is no fear in
love, but perfect love casts out fear. For fear has to do with punishment, and he who fears is not perfected in love. We love, because he
first loved us. If any one says, 'I love God,' and hates his brother, he
is a liar; for he who does not love his brother whom he has seen,
cannot love God whom he has not seen. And this commandment we
have from him, that he who loves God should love his brother also.

In the above the love of God has been defined in terms of
the life of Jesus. The act whereby God sent his Son into
the world to die for sinners has become the pattern, the
paradigm, of his love. For the early Church in general,
since the death of Jesus, the connotation of the phrase
'the love of God' had been historically conditioned or
illumined. The nature of God's love was seen in Jesus'
self-giving and the nature of our love to him came to be
understood in the same terms—in the love of the brother:
'If any one says, "I love God," and hates his brother, he
is a liar; for he who does not love his brother whom he
has seen, cannot love God whom he has not seen.' This
does not mean that love of God and love of man are
equated: this would be to empty the love of God of all
its numinous, awful nature. But it does mean that love
of the brother is the sure test of the true love of God.

To return again to our theme. The same orientation is
found in Paul: he seldom speaks of the love of God or of
loving God. He speaks of loving the neighbour in terms
of God's act in Christ. This is now for Paul also the
pattern of love and of life.

Rom. v. 6–8:

While we were yet helpless, at the right time Christ died for the ungodly. Why, one will hardly die for a righteous man—though perhaps for a good man one will dare even to die. But God shows his love for us in that while we were yet sinners Christ died for us.

Rom. viii. 32:

He who did not spare his own Son but gave him up for us all, will he not also give us all things with him?

Eph. v. 1 f.:

Therefore be imitators of God, as beloved children. And walk in love, as Christ loved us and gave himself up for us.

The most striking example of Paul's Christocentric understanding of love, however, occurs in 1 Cor. xiii, the hymn to love, which is probably to be understood as based upon a kind of character sketch of Jesus himself.

We can, therefore, claim that, like 1 John, Paul also urges us not so much to love our neighbour and to love God, as did Jesus, as to look at Jesus and then to love our neighbour in his light. Although the words of Jesus, as we have previously seen, are important for Paul, nevertheless this reference to Jesus means primarily participation in his life of self-giving: not listening to his words only or primarily but appropriating his life, death and resurrection is most emphasized.

This emphasis comes out most clearly, however, in the Fourth Gospel. While concentration on the act of God in Christ co-exists in Paul with reverence for his words, and while in Matthew the words of Jesus are given a prominence at least equal to his acts, when we turn to the Fourth Gospel we seem to be in a different world. Although John presents Jesus as a Rabbi and is careful to explain that the title 'Rabbi' as applied to Jesus was not a mere honorific but bore the connotation of 'teacher', nevertheless his attitude to the words of Jesus needs careful scrutiny. In the Fourth Gospel the title Rabbi is applied freely to Jesus by disciples and 'outsiders'; even the Risen Lord is addressed as rabbouni. That the Johannine Christ envisages his relation to his disciples somewhat after the manner of a Rabbi emerges clearly, and probably underlies John xiii. 1 ff. Moreover the verb to teach is used of Jesus in the same absolute way as in the Synoptics, without any indication being given as to the content of his teaching. In the Synoptics, and especially Matthew, it would appear that 'to teach' refers frequently to the ethical teaching of Jesus; but what is its reference in the Fourth Gospel?

In John xii. 23–6 we find an outcrop of the kind of ethical teaching which we encounter in the Jesus of the Synoptics: it inculcates self-sacrifice and reads:

And Jesus answered them, 'The hour has come for the Son of Man to be glorified. Truly, truly, I say to you, unless a grain of wheat falls into the earth and dies, it remains alone; but if it dies, it bears much fruit. He who loves his life loses it, and he who hates his life in this world will keep it for eternal life. If any one serves me, he must follow me; and where I am, there shall my servant be also; if any one serves me, the Father will honor him.'

But here the ethical teaching does not stand on its own feet: it is a kind of exegetical pendant designed to unfold the meaning of the hour, which has now come, in which the Son of Man is to be glorified (xii. 23). It is thus not introduced primarily for its intrinsic worth, but merely as explanatory of an event, the work of Jesus, his death. In vii. 14–24 we find a conflict story about Jesus and 'the Jews'.

About the middle of the feast Jesus went up into the temple and taught. The Jews marvelled at it, saying, 'How is it that this man has learning, when he has never studied?' So Jesus answered them, 'My teaching is not mine, but his who sent me; if any man's will is to do his will, he shall know whether the teaching is from God or whether I am speaking on my own authority. He who speaks on his own authority seeks his own glory; but he who seeks the glory of him who sent him is true, and in him there is no falsehood. Did not Moses give you the law? Yet none of you keeps the law. Why do you seek to kill me?' The people answered, 'You have a demon! Who is seeking to kill you?' Jesus answered them, 'I did one deed, and you all marvel at it. Moses gave you circumcision (not that it is from Moses, but from the fathers), and you circumcise a man upon the sabbath. If on the sabbath a man receives circumcision, so that the law of Moses may not be broken, are you angry with me because on the sabbath I made a man's whole body well? Do not judge by appearances, but judge with right judgment.'

The above is reminiscent of the kind of conflict which occurs in Mark and turns on the moral issue of healing on the Sabbath. But, apart from this, xii. 24 f. is the only passage in the Fourth Gospel outside the Farewell discourses where the ethical teaching of Jesus *as such* breaks through; and, as we saw, even here it is not neat. Similarly the application of the term *prophet* to Jesus does not connote any moral passion such as we usually associate with the term: it is his divinatory prowess in iv. 19, and in vii. 41 the mystery of his claims, rather than their ethical demand, that provokes the use of the term, while in vi. 14 and ix. 17 it is a 'sign' that calls forth the reference to a prophet.

And this last, like the subordination of ethical teaching to an event in John xii. 24 f., is typical, because, until we come to the Passion narrative, where the ethical demand of Jesus emerges unmistakably but in a peculiarly Johannine manner, it is the acts or signs of Jesus that are significant, not his ethical exhortation. In ii. 23 many believed because of the 'signs': there is no mention of the 'teaching'. In iii. 2 it is the signs which authenticate the divine origin of the teacher. So in v the ethical teaching is not mentioned. What provokes opposition is the alleged claim of Jesus to be equal with God (v. 19). It is given to the

Son not to teach, but to do and to judge, and the teaching of Jesus is not listed among those things which authenticate or bear witness to his claims. So in vi. 31 it is a work of Christ to which appeal is made, and in ix. 5 the important thing is to work the 'works of Him that sent me'. In x. 32 Jesus assumes that it is not his teaching, but one of his acts, that has caused Jewry to persecute him, just as it is his works that bear witness to him in x. 26, and that instigate faith in xi. 45 and opposition in xii. 37. The ethical teaching of Jesus, it would appear, does not constitute for the Fourth Gospel a *sign* of the Messiah as it does for Matthew and to a lesser degree for Mark.

This would seem to be reinforced when we ask what the exact content is of that teaching which is ascribed to Jesus in the Fourth Gospel. In iii entry into the Kingdom of God is not to be made a disciple unto it (Matt. xiii. 52) but to be born anew of water and the Spirit, and the content of the teaching of Jesus is conceived to be concerned with the revelation of 'the things above' (iii. 12, 26, 31). In vii. 28 f. the content of the teaching of Jesus turns out to be not an ethical demand but a revelation of his own origin; just as in viii. 29, 37, 47 the content is 'what His father has taught Him'.

And this leads to another emphasis in the Johannine presentation: the teaching of Jesus is markedly derivative. Waiving for the moment the meaning of the phrase 'But I say unto you' in the Sermon on the Mount, the teaching of Jesus in the Synoptics is stamped with his own authority. But the Johannine Christ in vii is careful to insist that he teaches only what has been given him to teach by the Father and in vi. 45 f. those who came to him are 'taught of God'. So in xiv. 10 the teaching of Jesus (his *rêmata*) leads to knowledge of the Father and is not his own (xiv. 24; xvii. 8, 14; xv. 10). In

iv. 41 the phrase 'they believed on account of His word' does not help us to fix precisely what the 'word' of Jesus meant; and again in v. 24 it is difficult to ascertain exactly what 'hearing the word' of Christ means. The phrase is parallel to 'to believe in Him that sent Me', so that it is probable that the 'word' connotes the revelation of God which Jesus has brought. Enough has been written to indicate that the words of Jesus on matters of conduct do not play in John the part they play in the Synoptics and especially in Matthew.

How is this fact to be interpreted, that the Fourth Gospel is apparently not concerned to indicate the moral teaching of Jesus as are the Synoptics? The suggestion is to hand that it had no need to do so because that teaching, by the time the Fourth Gospel came to be written, had become part and parcel of the Christian community. To recount the teaching was redundant. It is, therefore, perhaps because it assumes the awareness of that teaching that the Fourth Gospel 'ignores' it. But this is hardly a sufficient account of the matter, because the Fourth Gospel does assert the ethical seriousness of Jesus quite as strongly as Matthew, albeit in its own way.

In the first place, the Fourth Gospel sets Jesus *over against* Moses more explicitly than does Matthew, who sets them, as we saw, in parallelism. In the very first chapter, the Law, which had come through Moses, is contrasted with the grace and truth which came through Jesus, who is the exegesis of God, so to put it. And, elsewhere in John, Jesus appears not as the interpreter of the old Torah but as in his own person the Word, the Torah. Important is it to note that it is in the *person* and *acts* of Jesus more than in any synopsis of his words, such as we find in Matthew, that John finds Jesus as the Light, the Truth, the Way and the Word.

And, in the second place, John has summed up for himself the whole of the ethical teaching of Jesus in a 'new commandment'. This new commandment, however, finds its meaning not primarily, at any rate, in any words that Jesus uttered so much as in the love shown by Christ. It is the possession of this love rather than any training in the words of Jesus which constitutes discipleship.

John xv. 9–13:

As the Father has loved me, so have I loved you; abide in my love. If you keep my commandments, you will abide in my love, just as I have kept my Father's commandments and abide in his love. These things I have spoken to you, that my joy may be in you, and that your joy may be full.

This is my commandment, that you love one another as I have loved you. Greater love has no man than this, that a man lay down his life for his friends.

The new commandment corresponds with the commandment which Jesus had himself received from the Father (x. 18), which was that he should lay down his life; and it is this commandment which includes all the commandments which Jesus has to give (xiv. 15, xv. 20):

John xiv. 15:

If you love me, you will keep my commandments.

John xv. 20:

Remember the word that I said to you, 'A servant is not greater than his master.' If they persecuted me, they will persecute you; if they kept my word, they will keep yours also.

It is significant that the 'new commandment of love' occurs in the context of the Passion. This is fitting because the Passion itself is, for John, the most signal pattern of the new commandment. But not only so. Although there is no account of the taking of the bread and drinking of the cup at the Last Supper in John, the phrase 'the new commandment' may be taken to indicate that he too, like the Synoptics, thinks of the death of Jesus in covenantal terms: it inaugurates a new commandment for his own, illumined by his death.

And, further, the covenantal aspect of the death of Jesus is even more explicit in the reference to the 'blood and water' flowing from Jesus' side in xix. 34 (cp. Heb. ix. 19; which refers to 'blood, water, hyssop'. John mentions hyssop in xix. 29: contrast Mark xv. 36 which reads *kalamō*).

If we recapitulate, we now see that in the early Church there were various attitudes towards the actual ethical teaching of Jesus. For Paul, as for Matthew, the words of Jesus had an authority to which he submitted and to which he appealed for moral guidance. For the author of the Fourth Gospel, however, the words of Jesus on morals do not constitute, at least not explicitly, a court of appeal. Rather they are summed up in one commandment, which finds its connotation not in what Jesus said but in what he did, and particularly in the Cross. Matthew, we may further note, under the impact of those forces which we have previously discussed, has combined material of a radical kind with that of a regulatory kind to produce a new law which could be taught, we may now notice, catechetically. This is also true of the Epistle of James. We have next to ask whether in thus legalizing the tradition, as Paul had already begun to do before him, Matthew was departing from the mind of Jesus himself.

# THE SETTING IN THE MINISTRY
# OF JESUS

As we have seen in the preceding pages, Matthew drew around the figure of Jesus the mantle of a lawgiver. Certain elements in the primitive Church would have found this quite natural, and certain factors both outside and inside the Christian communities—anti-Paulinism, perhaps, Gnosticism of an incipient kind, sectarian infiltrations and the challenge of Judaism—may have stimulated this understanding of the Lord in Matthew. There remains to ask the question whether in thus rabbinizing Jesus, to use a loose term, Matthew has decked his Lord in an alien garb which falsifies the 'Jesus of History', that is, Jesus in so far as we can know him as he actually lived. Can we define the relation in which the Christ of the Mount stands to Jesus himself?

## A. *Transmission of his words*

Here those difficulties arise which we mentioned at the beginning of the first chapter. During the last two centuries we have witnessed the quest, for 'the historical Jesus'. The motive behind this quest, which largely dominated much NT scholarship both consciously and unconsciously for many decades, was the desire to be able to see Jesus of Nazareth behind and apart from the encrustations of Church tradition and dogma. But the labour devoted to it has had a very unexpected dénouement. Paradoxically enough, the outcome of the source and form criticism which it inspired has not been to lead us away from the 'traditional' Christ of the Church to a simpler, more probable and credible Jesus of history, as was often intended, but to engender the awareness that the very documents which are available for the quest are themselves so fashioned by the Church or Churches within which they arose that, in fact, it is only the Christ of the Church or the Jesus interpreted by the Church that we can know. To put it in other words, the Christ of the stained glass windows of tradition and dogma, to the destruction of whom so many books and sermons have been devoted, persistently re-emerges behind the dust of scholarship. The only changes in the picture seem to be confined to the background effects. These have recently taken on a far more Jewish colouring because we now know so much more about first-century Judaism. But the Jesus of history himself—so it is claimed—eludes us: we can only touch the hem of his garment. More pertinent to our immediate task is it that we can also only hear, so it is asserted, the whisper of his voice. The majority of the sayings ascribed to Jesus are sometimes stated to be the creation of the primitive Church. Hence it is not possible to discover what Jesus himself actually taught, but only what the early Church credited to him. And in this case the *SM* cannot fruitfully be discussed in its relation to the teaching of Jesus, since there can be no clear statement of this.

But the extreme scepticism which has often marked modern study of the life and teaching of Jesus is now being questioned. In connexion particularly with the teaching of Jesus, certain facts and probabilities should not be overlooked.

First, the milieu within which Jesus appeared was conditioned for the faithful reception and transmission of tradition. The phenomenon of the retention and repetition of sayings and speeches by worthy men in the Semitic world of the first and other centuries is familiar. To note one example, the laws now codified in the Mishnah were long preserved orally.

Secondly, the technical formulae describing the reception and transmission of tradition emerge so clearly in the NT documents that we must believe that the early Christian communities handed on a tradition. That this tradition included ethical teaching and not merely doctrinal truths appears clearly. Moreover, that this ethical teaching contained specific directions from Jesus himself is rendered certain for an early period by the fact that Paul used collections, oral or written, of the words of Jesus, which he sharply distinguished from his own opinions; and it is a fair assumption that Paul was not alone in making this distinction.

Thirdly, the claim that Jesus spoke most probably in Aramaic and that, therefore, since the tradition of his acts and words has come down to us in Greek, there is inevitably a certain falsification in the tradition (even though translation is notoriously interpretation, if not misinterpretation) must not be stressed. Apart from the possibility that Jesus *may* have been familiar with Greek, there were, from the earliest days of the Church, bilingual Christians to whom the translation of words from Aramaic to Greek would present no serious difficulty, so that the loss in authenticity incurred in translation should not be exaggerated.

Fourthly, it is highly pertinent to note that there was frequent intercourse between figures such as Peter, and other apostolic guardians of the tradition, and Christian communities in various places, so that the transmission and development of the tradition were not unchecked. It is not a vague folk tradition developing over vast stretches of time that lies behind the NT but an 'ecclesiastical' one which developed intensively in a brief period.

And, finally, there were specific interests at work in the early Church which would naturally have fostered the preservation of Jesus' words. While, therefore, it is idle to ignore that the tradition was influenced by the preaching, teaching, apologetic propaganda, catechism and liturgy of the Church, as the form critics have made luminously clear, and, furthermore, that the Church did very probably, if not certainly, ascribe to the Jesus of history words uttered under the influence of the Spirit, nevertheless, the actual words of Jesus had a fair chance of survival. Indeed, the very fact that the words uttered in the Spirit were ascribed to the Jesus of history, if such indeed were the case, is itself testimony to the seriousness with which the Church deemed it necessary to anchor its tradition in him. That there was a wholesale creation of sayings by the primitive communities, which were foisted on to the earthly Jesus, we should not assume. Far more likely is it that the Church inherited and preserved sayings of Jesus which floated in the tradition, modified them for its own purposes, and then, again, ascribed them to Jesus in a new form. The recognition of the original form may not be easy, but is also not always impossible.

So far, however, we have merely adduced general considerations to maintain that it is not unreasonable to claim that we may, after much sifting, be able to speak of the ethical teaching of Jesus and not merely of the early Church. Can we go further?

## B. *The Teacher*

Let us begin by insisting upon what may appear banal, namely, that Jesus of Nazareth was a teacher. That he was such is attested beyond dispute by the Fathers of the

Church, extra-canonical sources, and, particularly, the New Testament itself. We begin with the early Fathers of the Church.

The view is sometimes expressed that the weight of Christian devotion to Jesus soon proved too heavy to be expressed in terms of a pupil–teacher relationship and that as soon as Christianity encountered Hellenistic forces on any direct front the terms 'teacher' and 'disciples' proved inadequate: the name 'Christian' emerged at Antioch and the 'teacher' became a 'Lord'. But this is to overlook the fact that in the early centuries of the Church Jesus appears as the 'illuminator' and is frequently designated as 'teacher'. The evidence for this is plenteous. Of course, it is possible to argue that it was the Church that fabricated for itself the teaching that the Fathers ascribe to Jesus. But this would not invalidate their evidence as to the *propriety* of regarding Jesus as a teacher. Again, it is possible to dismiss the didactic emphasis in the Patristic understanding of Jesus, with which we are here concerned, as the intellectualizing of Christianity under the impact of Graeco-Roman culture; and to claim, for example, that when Clement of Alexandria speaks of Christ as teacher the term connotes not so much a source of ethical instruction as that of a saving mystery or *gnôsis*. But that the Hellenization of the tradition in Clement never went so far as to divorce it from its ground in Judaism appears from Clement's expectation of his Lord at His epiphany as 'teacher': that means that he is 'teacher' as judge: the ethical seriousness of the title is thus retained. The probability is that it is quite unnecessary to account for the Patristic emphasis by any extraneous influences: it is the natural continuation of an element already present, as we have seen, in the NT itself. That it became more marked in the Fathers is to be readily granted, but not that it indicates any peculiarity, in itself, of theirs or their decline.

The same understanding of Jesus as teacher emerges in the Jewish sources that refer to Jesus. When these are sifted they reveal Jesus as a crucified false teacher who had his disciples (*talmidim*). In one passage an actual word of his is cited, and it is possible that Christian emphasis on Jesus as an ethical teacher, who had his own interpretation of the Law, because he was the Messiah, led to the suppression of much Jewish speculation on the Messiah as the inaugurator of a New Law.

But, apart from such secondary sources, the evidence of the NT itself is quite unambiguous. He was addressed as teacher not only by his own disciples and by the public but by the learned themselves. He called 'disciples' to himself.

### C. *The eschatological Preacher*

At this point caution is necessary. Are we to think of Jesus as a rabbi or as some other kind of teacher? There were certainly many things which set him apart from the rabbis. The Synoptic tradition emphasizes the authority of his teaching: it differed from that of the scribes. Usually Jewish teachers had been the pupils of teachers from whom they had learnt faithfully that which they, in turn, transmitted to their own pupils. While they exercised great ingenuity in the exegesis of the Scriptures, their greatest respect was reserved for the virtue of faithfulness in handing on what had been received. But, as far as we know, Jesus had not been the pupil of 'teachers' other than those who may have taught him in the village school at Nazareth. And the 'authority' with which Jesus spoke constituted a problem to his hearers. He spoke with the authority of a rabbi, though he had not been taught or ordained: his authority was therefore not derivative but autonomous. How could this be, that an unlettered (*agrammatos*) man should know? The source of Jesus' authority in teaching, therefore, differs from that of the rabbis. It agrees with this that he expresses his teaching in the imperative, not in the participial form customary among rabbis, as does also the fact that, according to the tradition, He used Scripture as a witness to himself, which a rabbi would not normally do. And here it is that the content of Jesus' teaching perhaps most radically differs from that of the rabbis. If the tradition of scriptural exegesis which emerges so forcibly in the documents of the NT, whereby certain blocks of passages from the OT were applied to the life, death and resurrection of Jesus to illumine them, owes its initial impetus to Jesus himself, then it is clear that his attitude to exegesis was not altogether or even chiefly rabbinic. It is closer to that found in the Dead Sea Scrolls, where also Scripture is applied for the interpretation of historical events, and it implies a more directly personal involvement with the meaning of Scripture than was the case with the rabbis. This is explicable in the light of the understanding of his own ministry that Jesus possessed—that in his coming the Rule of God had drawn near. To this we shall return later.

And just as this eschatological awareness demanded of Jesus an exegetical orientation different from that of the casuistry of rabbinism, so it also dictated the external features of his teaching activity. Jesus not only taught in synagogues, but also in the open air by the sea and on the hills. His audiences consisted not only of pupils, members of his circle or 'school', though he had such, but also of the people of the land, publicans and sinners with whom he freely consorted. The nature of discipleship to Jesus has to be carefully noted, because it involved certain elements which differentiated it from the life of rabbinic students. Discipleship arose in response to a call from Jesus to follow him, a call directed to the individual in isolation or to hearers at large. By its very origin, therefore, it involved commitment of a personal kind to Jesus himself and to his service. It frequently meant the forsaking of home, kith and kin, wealth, comfort and security, and readiness to share in the way of Jesus himself, which was the way of the Cross. Thus in Luke xxii. 28 Jesus can describe his disciples as those who have continued with him in his trials. How does all this compare with that of a Jewish student? There may be instances of rabbis choosing their own pupils or encouraging 'bright young students' to sit at their feet, and rabbis are urged to raise up many disciples, but the Aboth advises an aspiring pupil 'to get him a teacher'. Akiba journeyed all the way from Babylon to Jerusalem to get him such an one in Hillel. The case of Akiba is also instructive in another way. For years, during his student life, Akiba was dependent on his wife for support, and, normally, preoccupation with the Law did not involve the severance of natural human ties. Many rabbis had secular callings, as did also their students. To become a student of the Law involved not so much a crisis, as did the call of Jesus, as concentration in study. And although the sacrifices made by the students of the rabbis for the sake of the Torah shine brightly, and although in times of persecution loyalty to their studies often meant death, nevertheless there was a marked difference between a life dedicated to study at the feet of a Rabbi, in which the aim was an increasing knowledge of the Law, which would eventually 'qualify' a student himself to become a rabbi, and the life of the Christian disciple (often not markedly studious by nature!) called to personal loyalty to Jesus in His way.

*not conformity but conversation*

For the one, the Torah is the ultimate concern, for the other, Jesus Himself. And it is this personalism also that made of the disciple of Jesus not another rabbi but an apostle.

### D. *The Rabbi*

We have above tried to do justice to the eschatological character of Jesus as teacher. But when all the differences between him and a rabbi have been noted and if it be admitted that in many ways Jesus was like a wandering Cynic-Stoic preacher rather than a rabbi or, more accurately, like a preacher from Galilee, one of the *ober Galilaea*, this must not be allowed to pre-empt him of all affinity with rabbis. For the rabbinic traits in Jesus are unmistakable also. He was called rabbi. While in his day the title may not have had the exact connotation of one officially ordained to teach that it later acquired, it was more than a courtesy title: it did designate a 'teacher' in the strict sense. Evidence of a rabbinic colouring in the activity of Jesus emerges also in the terminology employed of the disciples. A distinction is recognizable between 'coming to Jesus' and 'going after Jesus'. The last phrase is the equivalent of 'to follow Jesus'. When Jesus addresses the multitudes he invites them 'to come to Him': it is only the disciples themselves who can be said to follow. But the terms 'to come to' and 'to go after' are probably to be understood as the equivalents of rabbinic technical terms for going to a rabbi for instruction, and following a rabbi as his 'servant'. It agrees with this that in Mark xv. 41 (= Matt. xxvii. 55: compare Luke viii. 2 f.), 'to follow', which is the equivalent of 'to go after', is interpreted as 'to serve', which is an admirable translation of the rabbinic verb which is used of students being in attendance upon a scholar as disciples. The fact that in Mark xv. 41 those who serve are women does not make the terminology less significant, as we shall see below. The duties of a 'servant-disciple' are manifold. He brings his master's sandals, supports him at need, prepares his way for him, manages the ass on which he rides. A late passage defines the duties of a 'servant-disciple' as those of a slave except that he is not to take off his teacher's sandals: this last is reserved for the slave. It will appear that the functions of the disciples of Jesus in the Gospels are those ascribed to the 'servant-disciple'. The foot-washing scene in John xiii may have a side glance at the rabbinic custom. There Jesus repudiates the need for a 'servant-disciple' for himself and inculcates the same spirit for his disciples. There is a rabbinic parallel to this scene which shows that rabbis also could share in this spirit. Again, in Mark x. 45 the reference to the servant and the slave is instructive. Jesus seems here to be repudiating the reverential treatment meted out to the great: his terms may suggest rabbis. But this is unlikely because the context quite clearly has reference, not to rabbinic usage, but to Gentile. Moreover, Jesus seems to have accepted the honour ascribed to him, just as did the rabbis. Thus we are to understand in this light, probably, the service rendered to Jesus by Peter's mother-in-law and others. The service rendered is more than that at table: it belongs to the category of that rendered to great teachers even by their mothers and fathers.

Finally, we note that when Jesus taught he sat, as did Jewish teachers, and we may surmise that, despite the itinerary and 'crisis' character of his ministry, much of his time with his disciples went into the exposition of the Law. He was questioned in public about the Law and he was questioned in private. He was recognized by opponents as having the way of truth or at least as being able to discuss this; the reference in Mark xii. 14 f. is clearly sarcastic. The problems which emerge in the Gospels as having been dealt with by Jesus, for example, marriage, divorce, *lex talionis*, etc., are such as rabbis discussed. The extent to which the sources reveal an ability on the part of Jesus to use the rabbinic Hebrew of the schools must be a matter of conjecture. That he could hold his own with the learned emerges clearly and this presumably implies the ability to use their terms. On the other hand, it would appear that those technical terms which do emerge in the Synoptic accounts of discussions with learned opponents, for example, the practice of Corban in Mark vii, reference to which by Jesus has been taken to imply acquaintance with scholarly techniques, may have been so well known that no inference should be drawn from Jesus' allusion to it that he was technically learned. Again, other rabbinic terminology of an obvious kind occurs in passages which may not be authentic, for example, the phrase 'binding and loosing' in Matt. xviii. 15, xvi. 18. But the use of such terminology again demands no *particular* acquaintance with the methods of the schools. Subtlety, and a native wit, and awareness, the conflict of Jesus with his scribal, Pharisaic and other opponents reveals, but not necessarily the learning of the schools, although he could hold his own with scribal opponents, and must, therefore, have had a lively awareness of their method, if not an exact knowledge of it. The exegesis we find in Jesus' words is not casuistic in the rabbinic sense, but more in the nature of *pesher*, as we saw.

Nevertheless, the evidence presented probably justifies us in thinking of the Jesus of history as having a kind of 'school' around him: not a strictly rabbinic school but yet one that had rabbinic traits. Later on there was much in the structure of the Church that recalls the trans-

mission of tradition in Judaism: the impetus to this
development was already present in the ministry of Jesus.
We need not doubt that those chosen to be with him
learnt of him, treasured his words and passed them on.
The emergence of the words of Jesus in so many of the
documents of the early Church is not accidental: there
was a Christian tradition which had its point of departure
in Jesus of Nazareth himself, and whose 'continuity' was
preserved by the disciples of Jesus and their successors,
of various kinds, in the early Church. All of which makes
it credible that the 'words' of Jesus were preserved and
transmitted with some degree of faithfulness.

If what we have written above be accepted, then Jesus
of Nazareth appears in a twofold form, at least—as an
eschatological figure and as a rabbi, a teacher of morality.
As the oscillations in NT scholarship from Harnack to
Schweitzer show, the temptation is always present to
concentrate on the one to the neglect of the other: but
the two belong to one person. They may seem uneasily
yoked, but the conjunction to which we refer should not
be unexpected, because, in the Jewish hope for the future,
eschatology was never divorced from the ethical, the
Messianic King was to be also a teacher or interpreter
of the Law. The Messiah was to be like Moses perhaps.
And the same is true in the New Testament: Jesus as
Servant-Messiah had also to define his attitude to the
Law: *as the eschatological figure he was necessarily a teacher of
morality*. This appears clearly in the Marcan summary of
the Message of Jesus in i. 15: it reads, 'The time is fulfilled
and the Kingdom of God is at hand; repent ye and believe
the Gospel.' The proclamation of the eschatological event
calls for repentance: the act of God in the Gospel constitutes an appeal to man for a better life: the gift and
the demand are inseparable. And despite the modifications

introduced into his words by the Church, in view of that transmission of a tradition from Jesus through his disciples which we have indicated above it is a fair assumption that we can know what the moral teaching of Jesus, in its main emphases and intention, was. Let us now seek to establish this.

### E.  *The demand of Jesus in its setting*

To begin with, we have seen that Jesus of Nazareth appeared as a preacher of repentance. How did He conceive this repentance? It is sometimes stated that His call to repentance was not in terms of the Law. Is this view justified? Or was it not natural for him as New Moses to think of repentance in such terms? A comparison of Jesus with others who called for repentance in first-century Judaism may be instructive at this point. There were many such who thought of repentance in the light of the Law. The following factors are relevant.

The majority of Jews in the first century, we may assume, lived their lives in disregard of the claims of the Law. They constituted 'the people of the land' who were held in contempt by the religious. The circles from which Jesus emerged were not strictly speaking among 'the people of the land' in the technical sense. The whole of his dialogue with the Scribes and Pharisees makes it clear that he took the Law seriously. Whether Jesus intended to reject the Law we shall discuss below, but even if he did, which is unlikely, it was not from indifference to it, such as prevailed among 'the people of the land'. As we shall see, Jesus honoured the Law even while he struck it. For our present purpose, we merely have to note that 'the people of the land' do not at least directly illumine for us his call to repentance, except in so far as his call was directed to them with a sorrowful compassion and passion

unlike the passionate contempt often shown to them by
other religious leaders.

The second attitude to the Law in first-century Judaism
is that associated with the Sadducees. This was to accept
the written Law and the written Law only. They rejected
the authority of the oral tradition which had grown like
a fence around the Law itself. In one sense, in his critical
attitude towards the traditions of the fathers, Jesus is
near to the Sadducees. But whereas their rejection of the
oral tradition sprang from a rigid conservatism, which,
by insisting on the written Law only, virtually relegated
it to 'the museum for antiquities', Jesus rejected the
tradition of the fathers only to replace it by his own tradition or interpretation, so that he is both near to Sadducean
conservatism and far removed from it.

Next we come to the liberal approach of the Pharisees.
In their desire to make the Law relevant for the whole of
life the Pharisees accepted both the written Law and the
oral Law, which was its fence, as authoritative. Their
loyalty to tradition was the condition of 'adaptability'
in a changing world. They were concerned to apply the
Law to life (to judge from Finkelstein's treatment, at
least in the Spirit), much as Christian Socialists and
Liberals in our time have been anxious to apply Christianity to life. There is much evidence that Jesus for some
time sought to understand the Pharisees, and, in some
ways, He cannot but have sympathized with them.
Nevertheless, it was finally with the Liberal Pharisees
that Jesus was most in conflict because the very tradition
which they sponsored, as Jesus saw it, had ceased to
express the spirit of the Law around which it had grown,
and had, indeed, come even to annul its intention. This
is the force of Jesus' criticism of the Pharisees in Mark vii.
He rejected their kind of tradition. The call to repentance

uttered by Jesus was not the same, then, as that sent forth by the Pharisees: his demand for righteousness was to be greater and more exacting than theirs.

And, finally, we come to the group with which Jesus may have had, in one sense, most in common, and yet which he criticized, the Sectarians, whose literary remains have been recently discovered near the Dead Sea. Their attitude to the Law can best be described as *radical*. One of the key words they employed was the word *all*. 'All' the Law, as interpreted in the tradition of the Sect, was to be observed. To this end they forsook all, for a community 'in Torah and in wealth'. Here even more 'desperately'—a word which we use advisedly—than in Pharisaism the Law was interpreted and taken seriously. So seriously, indeed, that in no place do we find more agonized cries of unworthiness before the Law in pre-Christian Judaism than here: here is Judaism at its 'boiling point'.

Can we understand Jesus' call to repentance better in the light of that of the sectarians? These are not mentioned by name in the NT, but that John the Baptist had been influenced by them is probable, and Jesus himself, we may assume, knew of them. Like the sectarians Jesus issued a call to a radical repentance, for a decision in the light of an eschatological event, for obedience which was essentially moral and not cultic. Nevertheless, there is evidence that he criticized the Sect. As we saw, we can probably pin down this criticism explicitly to v. 43–8:

'You have heard that it was said, "You shall love your neighbour and hate your enemy." But I say to you, Love your enemies and pray for those who persecute you, so that you may be sons of your Father who is in heaven; for he makes his sun rise on the evil and on the good, and sends rain on the just and on the unjust. For if you love those who love you, what reward have you? Do not even the tax collectors do the same? And if you salute only your brethren, what more are you doing than others? Do not even the Gentiles do the same? You, therefore, must be perfect, as your heavenly Father is perfect...'

'Ye have heard that it was said, Thou shalt love thy neighbour and hate thine enemy: but I say unto you, Love your enemies.' This criticism occurs in that section where Jesus is giving his interpretation of the will of God and contrasting it with the understanding of *those of old*. And it is precisely at this point, that is, in the interpretation of the will of God, that Jesus differs from the sectarians. As we have seen, his 'personal' approach to the Scriptures was in a certain way like theirs, because the sectarians also applied the Scriptures of the OT directly to themselves. But whereas their understanding of the Law led them to an insistence on total literal obedience to their own understanding of the Law, which in turn meant entry into a closed community, governed by a rule which was uniform for all and which demanded hatred of those outside, Jesus had his own interpretation. He too demanded obedience to the will or Law of God, but, as he understood it, this was not an iron discipline equally applicable to all in a closed community but an all-inclusive love of the brethren and of those outside. Thus the difference between Jesus and the Sectarians was not in the intensity of the obedience they demanded: Jesus and the Sectarians are both 'totalitarians'. The difference between them lies in their interpretation of the will of God which demands this total obedience. They are alike in their radicalism but not in their understanding of the essential nature of the obedience demanded by God.

Can we reveal further the nature of this demand for Jesus?

Let us begin with the assertion that the Law and the Prophets of the OT remained valid for Jesus as the expression of the will of God: there is no complete break in Jesus with the ethical teaching of Judaism. The conflict stories at the beginning of Mark have given the impression that Jesus, from the very beginning of his ministry, was at daggers drawn with the teachers of his day. But this impression is to be resisted. There is much evidence that, as we saw, for a time at least Jesus and the Pharisees were not so opposed. The sources we possess for the ministry of Jesus emerge from a period when the Church and the Synagogue were increasingly diverging. But Jesus in his conduct seems to have been conservative. He appears in the Synagogue on the sabbath day, he joins pilgrims on feast days in Jerusalem, he is found in the Temple, he celebrates the Passover, he accepts the sacrificial rites and religious customs such as fasting, prayer and almsgiving. He wears the traditional dress of the pious: he is careful to recognize the rightful authority of the priest. With this it agrees that the early Church does not appeal to the practice of Jesus to defend its freedom from legal observance. Rather is Jesus, even for Paul, a minister of the circumcision born under the Law.

Thus Jesus was no iconoclastic revolutionary. He came not to destroy. On the other hand, he did come to fulfil. And there is much in his activity in the Gospels which suggests an attitude of sovereign freedom towards the Law. For example, his attitude to the sabbath appears to have been very free, as does his treatment of things clean and unclean. It is extremely doubtful whether at any point Jesus specifically annuls the Law. Thus in the discussions on the sabbath and on divorce he remains within the framework of the Law. At one point only can he be seriously considered to have destroyed the Law, in Mark vii, and on examination even this point is doubtful.

We shall, then, hold that the Law and the Prophets

remained valid for Jesus as the expression of the will of God. At this point he was at one with Sadducee, Pharisee, and Sectarian. Not his estimate of the Law as the revelation of the will of God set Jesus apart from these, but his interpretation of this revelation. In this sense there is a real continuity between his ethical teaching and that of the Law.

How did Jesus then regard the Law? In the Synoptic Gospels the ethical teaching of Jesus is presented in at least three contexts: in a context of doom, in a context of creation and in a context of Law. First, in a context of doom. The Gospels present Jesus as labouring under the conviction that the present order was to pass away either immediately or soon. In any case, he lived his life in the conviction that the End was at hand. And it has been claimed that it was this imminence of the End that enabled Jesus to shed all inessentials in his ethical teaching and to concentrate on the absolutely necessary demands of God: it was the light of the End that lent radicalism to his words and lit up for him the moral plight of man and his duty. Some have gone further and have said that it is only to the comparatively brief period that remained for him before the End of all things that his words were meant to apply. However, there is much in the teaching of Jesus which does not bear this character, but is clearly applicable to all times. Moreover, it is important to remember that it is highly questionable whether, in fact, an impending crisis does illuminate our present duty. The awareness of an imminent doom in itself may as much confuse as illumine as we, who face the Nuclear Dilemma, so-called, know only too well. The Sectarians at Qumran lived in the awareness of an impending crisis, but this led them to an increasingly rigid and narrow ascetic and withdrawn rigourism very different from the radicalism of

Jesus. Thessalonian Christians, who thought that the End of all things was at hand, promptly concluded that it was foolish to work. Those who calculated the times before the End, both in Judaism and Christianity, are not those necessarily most marked by ethical sensitivity. Even if Jesus did contemplate the End of all things soon, this in itself was not the secret of his illumination.

Next, we noted that his ethic is related to creation. We find in Jesus an appeal to the order of creation itself as a ground for morality, that is, an appeal to what was prior to the Law of Moses in time and rooted in the act of creation. Two sections, in particular, suggest this. There is first Mark x. 2–9.

And Pharisees came up and in order to test him asked, 'Is it lawful for a man to divorce his wife?' He answered them, 'What did Moses command you?' They said, 'Moses allowed a man to write a certificate of divorce, and to put her away.' But Jesus said to them, 'For your hardness of heart he wrote you this commandment. But from the beginning of creation, "God made them male and female." "For this reason a man shall leave his father and mother and be joined to his wife, and the two shall become one." So they are no longer two but one. What therefore God has joined together, let not man put asunder.'

Here Jesus' view of marriage and divorce is grounded in the very act of God in the creation of male and female. The purpose of God in creation is an indissoluble marriage, but the Law of Moses slipped in later, owing to the hardness of men's hearts, to allow divorce. Again the appeal to the natural order as a guide to the good life appears also in v. 43–5, vi. 26–32.

'You have heard that it was said, "You shall love your neighbour and hate your enemy." But I say to you, Love your enemies and pray for those who persecute you, so that you may be sons of your Father who is in heaven; for he makes his sun rise on the evil and on the good, and sends rain on the just and on the unjust...'

'...Look at the birds of the air: they neither sow nor reap nor gather into barns, and yet your heavenly Father feeds them. Are you not of more value than they? And which of you by being anxious can add one cubit to his span of life? And why are you anxious about clothing? Consider the lilies of the field, how they grow; they neither toil nor spin; yet I tell you, even Solomon in all his glory was not arrayed like one of these. But if God so clothes the grass of the field, which today is alive and tomorrow is thrown into the oven, will he not much more clothe you, O men of little faith? Therefore do not be anxious, saying, "What shall we eat?" or "What shall we drink?" or "What shall we wear?" For the Gentiles seek all these things; and your heavenly Father knows that you need them all...'

The same appeal is implied in the parables of Jesus, where a real correspondence is assumed between the natural and the spiritual world. This principle also played a prominent role in the early Fathers. Are we to conclude that it was Jesus who introduced this method of thinking about moral problems? This has been claimed, but there is the same appeal to the created order in the Zadokite Fragments, which probably belonged to the Dead Sea Sect, in a passage which, though written in Hebrew, strongly recalls Mark x: it reads:

The 'builders of the wall,' 'they that have walked after Zaw'—the Zaw is the preacher, as He has said: 'They shall surely preach' are caught in two *respects* in whoredom: (a) by marrying two women in their (masc.) lifetime, although the principle of nature is: 'a male and a female He created them...' (CDC iv. 21.)

And again in the Book of Jubilees laws are constantly based on the history of creation. Moreover, the OT itself finds a congruity between Nature and Man: for it too the good life is the 'natural' life, as for much of Stoicism: 'To live according to nature'—a Stoic phrase—is appropriate to the OT, as to Hellenistic sources.

Here again we must be careful, therefore, not to derive the peculiarity of the teaching of Jesus from any single principle such as 'the natural' or 'the created' to which

we have just referred. This principle is employed elsewhere, as we have seen, without producing that moral
illumination which we find in Jesus. Thus the Dead Sea
Sect appealed to the principle of creation, but did not
escape its terrible rigourism for that reason.

So we come to the third element detectable in the
teaching of Jesus: he sets his teaching in the context of
Law. Let us begin with the fact that, much debated as it
is, we shall assume, namely, that Jesus of Nazareth
thought of himself as the Messiah. But to say Messiah
is also to say Moses. The Messiah is Lawgiver, and Jesus,
if he thought of himself as Messiah, had to come to his
own terms with the Law. Both as Jew, and as Messiah,
the category of Law was not alien to him, as it is to us
modern Protestants, but native and congenial. And
although there can be little doubt that the Antitheses of
v. 22 ff. are the formulation of Matthew, there can be
equally little doubt that Jesus himself set his own teaching
in relation to the Law of his people. A good starting-point
is v. 48, which gives us an antithesis that probably goes
back to Jesus himself. Here the understanding of the love
of neighbour is taken radically by Jesus over against the
tradition of Qumran, which allowed, and, indeed,
demanded, hatred of those outside. The centrality of love
in the teaching of Jesus appears elsewhere in the Synoptics
in Mark xii. 28–34, Matt. xxii. 34–40, and Luke x. 25 ff.:

Matt. xxii. 34–40:

But when the Pharisees heard that he had silenced the Sadducees,
they came together. And one of them, a lawyer, asked him a question,
to test him. 'Teacher, which is the great commandment in the law?'
And he said to him, 'You shall love the Lord your God with all your
heart, and with all your soul, and with all your mind. This is the
great and first commandment. And a second is like it, You shall love
your neighbour as yourself. On these two commandments depend all
the law and the prophets.'

And while the commandment of love cannot be found frequently on the lips of Jesus himself, nevertheless, the NT as a whole makes it a justifiable assumption that this was a central theme of his teaching. (See my 'Ethics in the N.T.', *The Interpreter's Dictionary of the Bible*, 1962, vol. 1, p. 169.) The concept of love is undoubtedly the best summation of the ethical teachings of Jesus. It is customary to state that Jesus enlarged the understanding of the demand of Love in three ways: (1) by inseparably conjoining the love of God and man; (2) by reducing *the whole* of the demand of God to the twofold commandment of love of God and of neighbour He gave to these two commandments an unmistakable priority; (3) by extending the term neighbour to include everybody He universalized the demand of love. All this is true; but more important is it to recognize that Jesus revealed the nature of 'love' itself. I do not refer at this point to the use of the word *agapé* rather than *eros* in the NT, because the distinction usually insisted upon between these two terms cannot always be rigidly maintained. Rather do I think of the revelation of the nature of *agapé* vouchsafed to us in the pure, unlimited, self-giving which is exemplified by Jesus. 'Thou shalt love thy neighbour as thyself'—where the norm is the life and word of Jesus himself—is the commandment of the New Moses, the Messiah. And as Jesus radicalized love, so he radicalized the other demands of the Law, as is made clear in the Antitheses.

But we still have not answered the question as to how Jesus came to this penetrating understanding of God's will. Let us retrace our steps. As summarized in Mark, we saw above that the message of Jesus had two facets, the declaration that the Kingdom of God had drawn near and the call to radical repentance. And it is here, we suggest, that the secret of the radicalism of Jesus' demand lies. Not any imminent end of the universe, not any principle of creation, not any casuistry led Jesus to his understanding of God's will. He passed beyond all principles he had inherited, beyond the light of Law and Prophet, to what we can only call an intuitive awareness of the will of God in its nakedness. This awareness he expressed in terms of the imminence or presence of the Kingdom of God. We find in the Dead Sea Scrolls an awareness of the imminence of the End, but it is not expressed in terms of the Rule or Kingdom of God. The term the 'Kingdom of God' does not occur in the Scrolls, whereas in the Gospels it is ubiquitous. 'If I by the finger of God cast out demons, then has the Kingdom of God come upon you.' Whatever the actual teaching of Jesus about the future, the distinctive element in his teaching and activity was the realization that, in his ministry, the Kingdom of God was present. It is this that illumined him—his awareness of the Sovereign Rule of God in and through himself. This meant that whereas for Judaism the Law expressed the will of God, for Jesus his immediate awareness of the will of God became Law.

And this awareness, which lies behind his moral demand, raises the question as to who Jesus was that he had this awareness. This is another point at which the Dead Sea Scrolls are distinguished from the NT. They know no person who connected the Kingdom with himself, as did Jesus, and thus no ethic that passes beyond Scripture to the absolute will of God revealed to a person and in a person. Thus the expression of the absolute demand of God in the *SM*, as elsewhere in the NT, drives us back to the fundamental mystery of the person of Jesus himself. He himself in his own intuitive awareness of the will of God is the source of the radical ethic. His very words, therefore, point beyond themselves to himself, as their source: they too become witnesses to the King-Messiah.

We find there a reconciling principle. We noted previously that several strands co-exist in the moral tradition enshrined in the NT. The indicative strand, pointing to the life, death and resurrection of Jesus, to the act of God in Christ, as the root and pattern of all Christian living, appears in Paul, John and elsewhere. Similar to it is the emphasis on the imitation of Jesus, which also emerges in several places. These two strands, the indicative and the imitative, bid us look essentially to the fact of Christ. As the Epistle to the Hebrews puts it—'unto Jesus the author and perfecter of our faith' (xii. 1). But alongside these two emphases, we have also traced a fairly ubiquitous emphasis on the significance of the words of Jesus as such. But in the last resort these very words also compel us to ask: 'Who is this Jesus who thus speaks?', so that they too witness to him. They—the acts and words of Jesus—both compel the same question. They belong together as part of the ethic of Jesus and the mystery of his person. His words themselves confront us with him who utters them.

We are now in a position to answer the question whether Matthew, in concentrating on the words of Jesus as a 'new law', has departed from the mind of Jesus. The answer is both yes and no. In so far as he thereby recognizes that there is a demand, as well as a gift, at the heart of the Gospel, he remains true to Jesus. But by gathering together the words of Jesus and isolating them, to some extent, and presenting them as a unified collection constituting a 'law' in an external or independent sense, he has made it possible for many to isolate the ethical demand of Jesus from its total setting as part of the Gospel and has thus distorted awareness of that demand. But

certainly Matthew never intended to do this. We read the
*SM* in isolation from the grace of Jesus' ministry contrary to his purpose. In any case, the words of the *SM*
ultimately lead us back to him who uttered them. The
imperatives of the *SM* are themselves indicatives. And
we can go further: they are necessary to every indicative
in the NT. Emphasis on the act of Christ in life, death and
resurrection, central and essential as it is in all the NT, is
never wholly free from the danger of abstraction from
life. It is the penetrating precepts of Jesus that are the
astringent protection against any interpretation of that
life, death and resurrection in other than moral terms. In
this sense, the words of Jesus are part of the Gospel and
Matthew a true interpretation of the Lord's mind: the
Gospel is both gift and demand—a demand to be applied.

# 6

## CONCLUSION

Our examination of the historical setting of the *SM* is over, and it is well to record certain reflexions which it has provoked, because, although there are substantial signs of change, it might be claimed that such a strictly historical concern as we have above pursued stands outside the main stream of NT studies in recent decades, and that for obvious reasons.

On the one hand, literary disciplines have established for many that the Gospel tradition preserves only the whisper of the voice of Jesus. And, since to acquiesce in such a position is to imply that what that voice uttered is dispensable, a decline of interest in such passages as the *SM* was to be expected. On the other hand, with a few notable exceptions, interpreters of the NT have been largely absorbed in kerygmatic or strictly theological questions. The moral teaching of Jesus, although acknowledged, has been sharply distinguished from the kerygma of the Church and often treated as a Cinderella. Scholars have sometimes been even self-consciously anxious to relegate his teaching to a markedly subordinate place in the exposition of the faith of the NT. In particular, under the impact of a general revival of dogmatic interests, emphasis on Paulinism, often understood in terms of 'Justification by Faith Alone', as the most profound element in the New Testament, has made it difficult to do justice to other elements in which the demand of the Gospel, no less than its gift, emerges. The proper assessment of the relationship between Kerygma and Didache, Gospel and Law, has been jeopardized.

While our study has not presumed to deal with the
theological problems raised by the relation of Gospel and
Law, its pursuit could not but stir up the ghosts of these
problems, and it has inevitably reshuffled the data in
terms of which they must be approached within the NT.
Historical as is its intention, therefore, it is hoped that it
may not be without significance theologically. At least it
prompts the question whether history can sometimes be
called in to redress the balance of theology. To examine
the setting of the *SM* is to be compelled to recognize that
'these sayings of mine', 'the law of Christ', 'the new
commandment' played a more significant part in the NT
as a whole than is often recognized. The faith of early
Christians rested, not on a mime, but on a drama, and
in this drama the words of the protagonist on morality,
as on other subjects, were essential to the action. For some
in the primitive Church, if not for all, the penetrating
demands of Jesus, no less than the great kerygmatic
affirmations about him, were part of 'the bright light
of the Gospel', that is, they were revelatory.

NB    And not only so. However spontaneous its life in the
Spirit and 'revolutionary' its ardour, the stern realities
which confronted the infant Christian community, both
within its own ranks and in its encounter with Judaism
and the larger world, soon involved it in problems of law
and order. At this point, an instructive parallel with the
experience of the early Christian community is provided
by that of modern Russia. Parallels between Communism
and Christianity have frequently been drawn, but it has
seldom been noted how similar is their dealing with the
question of 'law'. Marx, and other socialist theorists,
approached this in two ways. First, they regarded the
traditional Russian legal system, like all existing legal
systems, as a cloak for class interest, a device which

reflected the claims of the bourgeoisie over against the propertyless masses. 'The economic structure of society', wrote Engels, 'always forms the real basis from which, in the last analysis, is to be explained the whole super-structure of legal and political institutions, as well as of the religious, philosophical, and other conceptions of each historical period.' And again, 'the jurist imagines that he is operating with *a priori* principles, whereas they are really only economic reflexes'. (Both quotations are taken from an unpublished work, by H. J. Berman of the Harvard Law School, *Comparison of Soviet and American Law*, 1961, pp. 9 f. There is a brief bibliography in another work, *Soviet Law in Action*, by Boris A. Konstantinovsky, ed. Harold J. Berman, Harvard University Press, 1953, p. v. I was introduced to Professor Berman's work by another Harvard lawyer, Mr C. Wadsworth.) But, secondly, in consonance with this, the same theorists looked forward to a future in which law, like the state, would vanish. In the new classless society, in which the proletariat would play a Messianic role, property relations would cease to exist, and thus the law and the state, which were designed to serve these, would no longer be neces-sary. There would be 'a glorious transition to a new order of equality and freedom without law' (Berman, *Comparison*, p. 24). Communism would be the end of law: it reveals on the question of law what a historian has referred to as a 'kind of New Testament foolishness' (p. 17). It is not surprising, therefore, that Soviet Russia, after 1917, passed through a period of legal nihilism. As late as 1930 a Soviet jurist was looking forward to 'the withering away of law in general, that is, the gradual disappearance of the juridical element from human relations' (cited by Berman, p. 21), and in 1927 a president of the Soviet Supreme Court wrote: 'Communism means not the

6

victory of socialist law, but the victory of socialism over any law, since with the abolition of classes with their antagonistic interests, law will disappear altogether' (cited by Berman, (p. 21)). And at first, after the Revolution, in accordance with Communist theory, law did tend to die out. But not for long could such a position be held. Already, before the above statements were written, under the brute actualities of Soviet life, there had begun a rehabilitation of law; the New Economic Policy adopted in the period 1921–8 meant, in effect, the restoration of 'bourgeois law'. The nihilism and apocalypticism which had sought for a society without law proved to be bankrupt, and a 'strategic retreat to law' the only possible policy (p. 21).

To compare the emergence of a vast modern state with that of the Christian Church may seem unrealistic. The parallel cannot be pressed because at no point in the Church, not even in Paul, who coined the phrase 'Christ is the end of the law', is there a radical rejection of the traditional law of Judaism but rather the recognition of its fulfilment in the 'law of love' and in the words of Jesus. The early Church was not iconoclastic: it refused to recognize legal nihilism. This was the only course possible for it, because, unlike Communism, it rooted the authority of the law, not in passing social structure, but in God, who could not be mocked. Nevertheless, within our immediate purpose, the parallel is illuminating. That the Church found it increasingly necessary to make the revelatory, radical, eschatological demands of Jesus the source of regulations is apparent. Convinced that they were living in the Messianic Age and yet compelled to recognize that that Age had not reached its consummation, Christians had to face moral problems which demanded a Christian way to meet these. Some did this, not only by grounding

imperatives in a kerygmatic indicative, but also by turning to the words of Jesus as their 'law' and the ground of a
new casuistry. The fullness of the time had indeed come,
but law was not dispensable. It is the reality of this state
of affairs in its many ramifications that this study has
revealed. To interpret the faith of the NT only, or even
mainly, in terms of a rigid understanding of the Pauline
antithesis of Grace and Law is to ignore not only the
tumultuous, tortuous nature of Paul himself (a fact which
alone should make us chary of making his experience in
any way normative), and not only the exaggerations
engendered by the historical controversy out of which
that antithesis arose, but, even more, much evidence
pointing to a 'law' which remains in the new covenant
of grace, and, indeed, especially there, and which is
rooted in the words of Jesus Christ himself.

A historical approach, such as we have attempted
above, therefore spurs the question anew whether, in
the matter of Gospel and Law, the gulf fixed in the subsequent life of the Church between Protestant and Roman
Catholic, Lutheran and Calvinist, cannot be bridged in
terms of the wholeness of the NT, the fragmentation of
Christian history being healed there. Certain it is that
the *SM* in its setting spans the arch of Grace and Law,
conjoins demands such as those of 'the right strawy
Epistle' of James with the Pauline profundities. Its
opening, the Beatitudes, recognizes man's infinite need
for grace, his misery; its absolute demand recognizes
man's infinite moral possibilities, his grandeur. Thus it is
that our effort to set the *SM* historically in its place finally
sets us in our place. And the place in which it sets us is the
Last Judgement, before the infinite succour and the
infinite demand of Christ.

*and all this from a Protestant!*

# INDEX OF REFERENCES

*Bold figures refer to pages where extracts appear*

### A. THE OLD TESTAMENT

## B. THE APOCRYPHA AND PSEUDEPIGRAPHA OF THE OLD TESTAMENT

## C. THE NEW TESTAMENT